JUMPING FOR
JOY

Much Love in Jesus!

Joy Smith Griffin

Mt. 5:6

Rom. 10:13-15

Eph. 3:14-21

JOY SMITH GRIFFIN
AS TOLD TO JAN DE CHAMBRIER

Printed in the United States of America

First Printing, 2020

ISBN: 978-0-578-80597-9

To my husband, Wes,
and our children, Hannah and Caleb—
my greatest treasures from God.

CONTENTS

ACKNOWLEDGMENTS

*"God always has a purpose bigger than you and
me in mind. He is out to save His world!"*

DR. DENNIS KINLAW

This book has been written with purposes bigger than me in mind. My goal is to remind others of God's awesome display of power—to testify that Jesus continues to do the miraculous today, just as He did in the Bible. My hope and prayer is that it will be a witness to just a few of the amazing things God has done, and is doing, in His world.

These pages would not be possible without the influence of those who have nurtured and discipled me through the years—family, friends, and neighbors whose love and encouragement spurred me on to pass along what I have learned and experienced.

My spiritual sister, Jan de Chambrier, has labored to tell my stories in beautiful ways, so the reader can "see" what I'm trying to say. I am so grateful for her extraordinary giftedness and discerning heart. Jan wrote what I wanted to convey, but did not have the words to express. She is amazing! She did not change my stories at all, but made them come to life for the reader!

I'm so thankful for layout designer Sandy Jurca, who has made my words appealing to the eye. Her talent is incredible!

My gratitude to my friend, Katie Bennett for using her creative skill to arrange the cover art. Janet Thornbrough, Cricket Albertson, and Judy Seitz gave their time to read the manuscript for grammatical errors and story flow. I am so grateful for their friendship, giftedness, and willingness to help me.

Most of all, my gratitude overflows to Him who gave me the gift of physical life, the gift of hunger for abundant life here on earth, and the indescribable gift of eternal life in His presence. I praise Him!!!

ABOUT THE COVER ART

Atlanta-based artist HANNAH GRIFFIN painted the beautiful depiction of God's creation gracing the cover of this book. Using a photo taken of me jumping for joy on a mountain in Patagonia, South America, Hannah—my beautiful daughter—recreated this magnificent scene in acrylics. Hannah also came up with the title of this book, *Jumping for Joy*.

Here is some information about Hannah if you'd like to know more about her work.

Hannah Griffin creates abstracted, expressionistic repro-ductions of photographs through vibrant colors and bold brush strokes. Working year-round on custom commissions, she paints portraits of loved ones, landscapes, animals, florals, abstracts, and shirt designs. Available to paint in person at wedding ceremonies and receptions, churches, and corporate events, Hannah has also worked with companies including CONA Services (Coke One North America) and Orvis.

Hannah's commissioned pieces are displayed at the Carroll County (GA) Court House, and County Agriculture Center, as well as the Tanner Medical Center in Carrollton, GA—the same hospital where she was born. Hannah was blessed to work for well-known artist Steve Penley during her college years, and graduated with a Bachelor of Fine Arts degree in painting from the University of West Georgia before launching her private art studio.

For additional information, please visit
hannah@hannahgriffinart.com

Samples of her work can be found at:
Facebook: Hannah Griffin Art
Instagram: hannahgriffinart
www.hannahgriffinart.com

PREFACE

For many years, people have urged me to write a book about my personal testimony and missionary journeys around the world, but the timing was never quite right. I'm an action person, and the thought of the hours, days, weeks, probably even months it would take to sit down and write a book seemed like more than I wanted to undertake. Still, I knew it was something I needed to do because the stories of what Jesus has done need to be shared.

In November of 2016, my dear friend Jan de Chambrier and I spent two weeks together in the Holy Land, leading conferences together for women in Israel and Palestine. As we shared our hopes and dreams, I told her about my desire to write a book about all the incredible things Jesus has done throughout my life. Jan, a published author, urged me to do this, saying, "Joy, the world needs to hear your stories. When the time is right, let me know and I'll help you."

Knowing very little about the process of writing and publishing a book, the prospect intimidated me, but I sensed an urgency to follow through with the prompting of the Holy Spirit. After doing some preliminary research, I called Jan in July, 2020, having recalled our conversation of four years ago. She immediately said with great excitement, "Joybells, my offer is still good! Let's do it!"

Understanding my personality, Jan suggested I record my stories by voice memo and she would then transcribe and write them. One by one, I recorded the miraculous testimony of how Jesus completely healed me from paralysis after I received the second work of grace—the presence and power of the Holy Spirit; my years at Asbury Seminary, preparing for ministry; meeting my husband Wes, and how the Lord led us to marry and minister together to the nations; raising our beautiful children, Hannah and Caleb; going out to the uttermost ends of the earth to preach and teach the gospel.

While some might use the term *ghostwriter* to describe what Jan has done, the only "ghost" involved was the Holy Ghost—the Holy Spirit. Jan explained to me that she had asked the Holy Spirit to sanctify her imagination and write my stories through her. Since she has traveled to many of the same parts of the world as I, she was able to describe places and people in a firsthand way. My stories themselves are factual in testimony; there is nothing fictional other than the myriad descriptive details Jan uses to help the reader feel as if they were eyewitnesses to each story. We have also changed some names in order to protect identities of vulnerable parties in persecuted countries.

Every story begins and ends with a passage from the Word of God, the Alpha and Omega. May these testimonies of Jesus inspire and encourage you to fulfill every plan and purpose He has for your life. May Jesus Christ be praised!

"COME AND SEE!"

"COME AND SEE!"
PART ONE

Now Peter and John went up together to the temple at the hour of prayer, the ninth hour. And a certain man lame from his mother's womb was carried, whom they laid daily at the gate of the temple which is called Beautiful, to ask alms from those who entered the temple; who, seeing Peter and John about to go into the temple, asked for alms. And fixing his eyes on him, with John, Peter said, "Look at us." So he gave them his attention, expecting to receive something from them. Then Peter said, "Silver and gold I do not have, but what I do have I give you: In the name of Jesus Christ of Nazareth, rise up and walk." And he took him by the right hand and lifted him up, and immediately his feet and ankle bones received strength. So he, leaping up, stood and walked and entered the temple with them—walking, leaping, and praising God. Then they knew that it was he who sat begging alms at the Beautiful Gate of the temple; and they were filled with wonder and amazement at what had happened to him.   ACTS 3:1-10, NKJV

HAVE YOU EVER WONDERED whether such phenomenal miracles could still take place today? Well, have I ever got a story for you! This little gal from a dairy farm in west

Georgia understands firsthand what can happen when Jesus gets ahold of your heart.

Our little country church was the center of my world growing up. My parents, brother, and I were at every service, hymn sing, potluck supper, wedding, and funeral the church had to offer. Since it was in such a rural area and so tiny in numbers, we tended to have student pastors, young seminarians who would drive back and forth from Atlanta to practice their preaching.

Like several of my friends, I had asked Jesus to come into my heart at church camp the summer I was twelve years old. There was lots of emotional enthusiasm as we lifted our hands up high, praising Jesus and agreeing on how wonderful it was to know we were saved and wouldn't be going to hell when we died. But alone, in the privacy of my own room, my heart didn't feel exactly right. Somehow, I sensed there was a whole lot more I needed to know about following Jesus.

At night, as I lay sweltering in my little room, listening to the crickets and katydids singing their evening serenades, my own song felt like a psalmist's lament. I would think about what Jesus said in the Bible, and bemoan the fact that so many things in my life didn't seem to measure up to what He taught. I thought of Jesus hanging on the cross between the two criminals, talking to His Father about them. *"Father, forgive them, for they know not what they do"* (Luke 23:34). Suddenly, I started bawling, realizing I honestly didn't know how to forgive others.

As the penetrating power of the Holy Spirit washed over me with quiet yet deep conviction, I began thinking of all the times I had held grudges when others did something to offend me. Things like someone blocking a shot I was trying to make at a basketball game, or my brother taking the last piece of peach cobbler (although anyone reading this who ever tasted my momma's cobbler totally understands it was something worth fighting for), or any number of little slights that caused me to nurse a grudge. My heart wasn't clean and I didn't want it to stay like that. I knew I needed to find someone to help me, some kind of spiritual authority I could talk to about the sorry state of my heart.

Thinking someone who was in seminary would know how to fix my dilemma, the following Sunday, I grabbed my Bible and went to see the student pastor.

"Pastor, um . . . I need to get something off my chest. I, uh, when I read the Bible, I'm noticing my life doesn't look much like Jesus. I need help. I really don't understand how to love God. I don't know how to forgive others. I want my heart to be right."

Looking at me with a tinge of amusement in his eyes, the young student pastor said, "Joy, you're about the best person we know! You're just having an emotional reaction. Don't worry about it; you'll feel better in the morning."

Well, I'd never heard that particular prescription for spiritual heartache, either before or since; he may just as well have told me to take two aspirin. It wasn't until years later that I would understand why he couldn't help me with my problem. He did not understand the person of the Holy Spirit.

Feeling ashamed of how I felt, yet unable to fix it by myself, my teen years flew by, my problem still hovering in the wings. I graduated from college, looked for a job, and then faced a major life decision. Should I accept the job I had been offered, or should I enroll in seminary and try to find the answer to the endless ache I felt in my heart? Seminary won out.

Having been sheltered in my little country church and high school, never really exposed to different ways of thinking, the terms "liberal" and "conservative" meant nothing to me. I figured I'd just enroll in the seminary closest to home so I could commute and save the cost of room and board. So, I joined a carpool with four more-experienced seminarians and started classes there that fall.

With an hour-and-a-half drive each way, there was lots of opportunity to get to know the guys in the carpool. One of them said that first day, "Joy, what made you decide to go to seminary?" At the time, there weren't a whole lot of women in that field.

I replied, ever so earnestly, "I'm searching for more of God."

After a few moments of respectable silence, one said, "Well, Joy, I think we're probably all looking for that, but we basically just preach about peace and figure we'll find the rest when we get to heaven." My inner self gasped. How pathetic was that?!

With each passing day, my confusion and inner turmoil only grew. Having enrolled in a class called "The Theology of Paul," I had been excited to learn more about the apostle who wrote the majority of epistles in the New Testament. But with every class, the professor would read in a banal tone of voice from the letters of Paul in the original Greek, not exactly communicating in a way I, or probably any of my classmates, could understand.

Asking my carpool cohorts about this professor and his off-putting approach to teaching, they said, 'Oh, he claims to be an atheist."

"What?!" I cried indignantly. "How can someone who doesn't even believe in God teach at a seminary?"

Since no one had ever dared ask the professor that pivotal question, the four of us conspired with others in our class to find out. As one brave soul volunteered to do the dirty work, the rest of us promised that, if our classmate were to fail this course as a result, all of us would go down with him.

The appointed day arrived, and our courageous comrade boldly asked, "Professor, there are rumors going around that you are an atheist."

Without missing a beat, the man said, "That is correct."

"How can you teach in a seminary and not believe in God?" our friend persisted.

With no apologies whatsoever, the professor said, "Two reasons. One, this is a very prestigious school and they pay me a (curse word) of a lot of money. Two, I have tenure and they can't fire me." Case closed.

Incredulous, feeling sick to my stomach, I wondered what kind of hornet's nest I'd gotten myself into. My hope of finding a spiritual authority at that school who could help me figure out my own heart was dashed that day. But I couldn't—I wouldn't— give up.

About four weeks into the semester, our women's softball team had made it into the championship game and we were in the bottom of the ninth inning, up by just one run. We had two outs on the other team, but needed one more out to win the game. The problem was there were runners on second and third bases, so if the ball got through the infield on the ground, it would be all over for my team and the coveted championship. With victory so near I could just about taste it, I was hoping for an easy out with a strike-out or pop fly. But when the ball was pitched, the ace batter connected with a magnificent, rocket-like line drive that was great for the other team but doomsday for ours. Still, I knew there was one last chance, if only I could run fast enough to catch that ball!

I dove into the ground, similar to the way you'd slide into first. Plopping soundly into my glove like ice cream into a cone, that ball and I melded together. We WON! Even as the crowd leapt to their feet and erupted with cheering, my momentary elation was quickly eclipsed by a searing pain and the sudden awareness that I was trapped on the ground, immobilized in my own body.

Instantly paralyzed, I was at the mercy of those around me who rushed to my side. I don't recall many details because of the shock that temporarily kept me from realizing the desperation of my circumstances, but I do remember the doctors telling me I would never walk again. When I fell, the trauma caused the muscles, nerves, and bone tissue to rip away from my spine, leaving everything inside me in one big, tangled jumble. The internal trauma was so deep that it even caused my monthly periods to stop.

Crushed emotionally as well as physically at the tender age of 22, I tried to wrap my head around the devastating reality that I would never walk down a church aisle to meet my bridegroom. I would never cradle a newborn baby in my arms. I couldn't even do something as basic as use the toilet. A bedpan became my constant companion next to the pallet that my mother arranged for me on our living room floor.

As distressed as I was by physical infirmity and relentless pain, my most tormenting thought was, *Now I'll never even be able to go out and find someone to help me understand how to become like Jesus.* What I didn't take into account was that Jesus wanted for me to know Him even more than I did. He had already set a plan in motion that would forever transform my life. He was sending someone to help me.

~

Fear not, for I am with you; be not dismayed, for I am your God. I will strengthen you; yes, I will help you.
I will uphold you with My righteous right hand.

ISAIAH 41:10, NKJV

"COME AND SEE!"
PART TWO

Call to Me, and I will answer you, and show you great
and mighty things, which you do not know.

JEREMIAH 33:3, NKJV

SOME PEOPLE JOKINGLY refer to Jeremiah 33:3 as God's
phone number, but I can sure tell you He answered my call
and dispatched a messenger just for me who would teach
me from the Word. Even though our little country church
typically used young seminarians who would serve for a
time as they went through school, in the months following my accident, the pattern abruptly changed. An older
gentleman, the Rev. Howell Hearn, had just retired but still
wanted to serve the Lord in ministry. Having grown up in
our area, he and his precious wife, Velma, moved back and
began serving in my home church, New Hope.

Faithful to minister to the elderly and shut-ins, Pastor
and Mrs. Hearn would make their daily rounds to nursing
homes, hospitals, and to those like me who needed prayer
and care in their homes. Having no idea their visits would
change my life forever, they knocked on the door of our
farmhouse and were warmly greeted by my sweet momma.

"Joy, you have some visitors! The pastor and his wife
would like to see you," she announced as I was lying

forlornly on my pallet on the living room floor. Since I hadn't been able to go to church for several months, I had no expectation of anything other than perhaps a sympathetic acknowledgment of my pathetic predicament and a polite little prayer.

But looking up as they entered the room, I saw a kind of glory light emanating from them that I had never seen before in anyone else. Later on, I would know it was the *shekinah* glory, the divine presence of the Lord Jesus, shining through them, reflecting His radiance. But I knew right then, whatever it was, it was glorious—and I wanted what they had.

Dressed as simple country folk, he looked every bit like a gentleman farmer in his plaid shirt and dungarees; she wore a simple gingham housedress like the other women in the countryside. There was nothing physically outstanding that would draw attention to them. But Pastor Hearn's humble demeanor couldn't disguise the power of God residing in him. With a deep, rich, bass voice, he peered down at me and said, "Well now, tell me how you're doing."

I figured since he was a pastor, I'd better just come out with the truth. "I'm miserable," I moaned.

"Oh, Joy, that's good!" he said.

Thinking he must be either deaf or senile, I kind of yelled back up at him, "No, sir. Did you *hear* me? I'm MISERABLE!"

"Oh, Joy, that's gooood, because Matthew 5:6 says, *Blessed are those who hunger and thirst for righteousness, for they shall be filled.* I know that you're hungry, and when you're hungry, Jesus can fill you. Jesus also says in Matthew

5:8, *Blessed are the pure in heart, for they shall see God.* And He tells us, *If you search for me with all your heart, you will truly find me* (Jeremiah 29:13). And Hebrews 12:14 says, *Without holiness, no man will see the Lord.* This is good, Joy! You're hungry and you're looking for Him!"

Well, it sure sounded simple, almost too simple. I'd been hungry for years. I'd looked everywhere I knew to look. And here was this man telling me my misery was *good*! But because of the light I saw shining through him, I thought I'd better listen to what he had to say. So, I started asking questions, hoping he would be able to give me some answers.

"So how do I do that, get filled?" I asked in a pretty tenuous voice.

"Oh, that's *easy*, Joy!" Smiling down at me with an almost mischievous grin, I somehow sensed this man had some secrets to share with me that would one day unlock the door to my heart. "Just give everything to Jesus."

"But I *did* that when I was twelve!" I protested. Feeling just a little guilty that maybe I was stretching the truth a little, I figured it was probably impossible to give *everything* to Jesus. After all, we're only human. And in school, 98% or 99% is still an A plus!

But suddenly the words to the old hymn by Judson Van DeVenter, *I Surrender All*, came to mind. In fact, I could visualize it in the Cokesbury hymnal, I think it was #148 or 149:

All to Jesus I surrender, All to Him I freely give;
I will ever love and trust Him, In His presence daily live.

I surrender all, I surrender all;
All to Thee, my blessed Savior,
I surrender all.

With that conviction, I agreed to let Pastor Hearn teach me every day from the Scriptures. With his booming bass voice, this man might have been intimidating, but his spirit was so filled with Jesus that everything he said, no matter how much it may have pierced my soul, always came across as gentle and kind. I knew he wanted God's best for me.

"Joy, you have to understand that there are two kinds of sin. The first kind, *sins* in the plural, is actually the outward effect or result of the action of sinning. But the real problem, the problem you're struggling with right now, is the second kind of sin, which is *sin* in the singular. This is what is sometimes called the flesh or carnality; it's our sinful nature. It is the same spirit that caused Adam and Eve to disobey God in the Garden of Eden, and the same spirit that has afflicted every human being ever since. It is pride and ego, the spirit that causes you to commit the outward actions that we call sins."

This was a revelation to me, understanding that it wasn't just my own personal problem but the problem of humanity in general. Pastor Hearn went on to explain, "The only solution is sanctification, being washed and cleansed and purged and purified by God." This was a bit confusing to me, since I thought sanctification was just a fancy word for salvation, and I knew I already had that. But as he explained more to me from the Scriptures, it started to make sense.

"Joy, think of Psalm 51 where David says, *In sin my mother conceived me. Behold, thou desireth truth in the inward parts, and in the hidden part Thou shalt make me to know wisdom. Purge me with hyssop, and I shall be clean; wash me, and I shall be whiter than snow. Make me to hear joy and gladness, that the bones which Thou hast broken may rejoice. Hide Thy face from my sins, and blot out all mine iniquities. Create in me a clean heart, O God, and renew a right spirit within me*" (Psalm 51:5-10, KJV).

Well, I could sure relate to those bones that needed to rejoice, and I really did want a clean heart in me. But I thought of the friends I had at that time, which was the beginning of the Charismatic Movement, when people were experiencing signs and wonders and speaking in tongues. They seemed to want more of Jesus, too, but their lives really didn't look any different from mine. I wanted to look like the Jesus in the Bible.

"Pastor, why is it that my friends speak in tongues and lift their hands up, but I don't really see any difference in the way they live?" I asked.

"Joy, think of who Jesus is. Scripture says He is the exact representation of the Father (Hebrews 1:3). We also know that Jesus told His disciples that He would be sending them another just like Himself: an Advocate, a Comforter, the Spirit of truth, who would be with them. And that is who we know as the Holy Spirit, the fruit of the life of Jesus that comes to live in us when we ask Him.

"Imagine Him holding your heart right now in His hand. God's Word promises that He will cleanse your heart of all unrighteousness if you offer it to Him, but then that heart remains empty until Jesus fills it with the fruit of His Spirit. So, until He pours into your empty heart the fruit we know from Galatians 5:22-23—love, joy, peace, patience, kindness, goodness, faithfulness, gentleness and self-control—you will still have a longing for your heart to be filled."

That made me think of Jesus as a fruit tree, with all the branches representing the fruit of the Spirit. I desperately wanted that, but still didn't know how to get it. But I felt like maybe I was getting closer. Just maybe my fruit tree had a few little buds on it.

Day after day, Pastor Hearn would come to disciple me, just like it says in Isaiah 50:4. *He awakens me morning by morning; He awakens my ear to listen as a disciple* (Berean Study Bible). I just got hungrier and hungrier for that fruit to come into my life and satisfy me. One day, he explained to me what it means to be sanctified, to be made whole in every part, as Scripture speaks of in I Thessalonians 5:23-24. *Now may the God of peace Himself sanctify you completely; and may your whole spirit, soul, and body be preserved blameless at the coming of our Lord Jesus Christ. He who calls you is faithful, who also will do it* (NKJV).

"Jesus is holy, just as God is holy. God talks about holiness a lot in the Scriptures, beginning in Genesis, certainly highlighted in Leviticus, the Psalms, Isaiah, and appearing again many times in the New Testament. I Peter 1:16, *Be ye holy; for I am holy,* even quotes Leviticus 20:26. God is very serious about holiness."

This word scared me for some reason. The idea of holiness conjured up images of snake charmers, probably a product of my overactive childhood imagination. But once again, remembering the old hymns I'd sung over and over at our little country church from the Cokesbury hymnal helped remind me of the truth. I thought of *Holy, Holy, Holy,* maybe it was #6 in the hymnal, written almost 200 years ago by Reginald Heber.

Holy, holy, holy! Lord God Almighty!
Early in the morning our song shall rise to Thee.
Holy, holy, holy! Merciful and mighty!
God in three Persons, blessed Trinity!

But verse three was the real clincher:

Holy, holy, holy! Though the darkness hide Thee,
Though the eye of sinful man Thy glory may not see,
Only Thou art holy; there is none beside Thee,
Perfect in power, in love, and purity.

There were two of those key words Pastor Hearn had been talking about: sin and purity. The first was my human nature, and the second was the nature of God, the holy one. Pastor had told me that to be holy was to be surrendered, set apart, belonging completely and solely to Jesus, with every part of me made whole.

I thought of the passage in Isaiah 6:1-8 where the prophet sees a vision of the Lord seated on a throne, with His train filling the temple. The seraphim surrounding the throne are crying out, *"Holy, holy, holy is the Lord of hosts; the whole earth is full of His glory!"* Isaiah is completely undone by the awareness of his own sin, but a seraphim touches his mouth with a searing hot coal from the altar and says, *"Behold, this has touched your lips; your iniquity is taken away, and your sin purged."*

Then Isaiah hears the voice of the Lord saying, *"Whom shall I send, and who will go for Us?"* And he answers, *"Here am I! Send me."* I guessed this must be what holiness was all about. But I still didn't quite know how to get there. So near, yet so far.

Feeling a bit overwhelmed and inadequate, I figured I might just as well be honest with him. I said, "I want to believe you, but I need you to prove it to me."

"Joy, think of the many descriptions of God in the Old Testament: our Father, Protector, Provider, Shepherd, Just Judge, Healer, and so many others. Think of Jesus in the New Testament, who is in His very nature God, with the same attributes as His Father. And now think of what Jesus promised His frightened disciples in the Upper Room on the night on which He was betrayed. We have the account in John 14 where He reassures them that, even though He would be leaving them for a little while to go and prepare a place for them, He would be coming back. And what's more, He told them they wouldn't be left as orphans; He would ask the Father to give them another Helper. This Helper is the Holy Spirit."

While I knew these things from my study of Scripture, suddenly my eyes were opened to imagine how the disciples, many of them as young as I was, must have felt that night, knowing their leader and best friend would soon be leaving them. Growing up in Sunday school, I had always thought the Twelve were like superheroes of the faith, not real people with real problems and the same sinful nature as the rest of us. Since they had left everything to follow Jesus, I figured they knew what it was to surrender all. But Pastor Hearn spoke of their frail humanity that reminded me so much of my own.

"Even though the disciples left homes and family and jobs to follow Jesus, they were real human beings, just like us. They worried about where their next meal was coming from and how they would feed the multitudes. They were overly impressed with position and money, wondering why Jesus would turn away a rich young man who wanted to join their ranks, knowing they could have used his bank account to finance their ministry. They were annoyed by all the little kids who wanted to come to Jesus, thinking they were a nuisance. They were impatient with some of the crazy people who needed to be delivered from demons. They didn't really understand forgiveness and wanted a formula to know when enough was enough.

"Even after three years of living daily with Jesus, their human nature was still showing. The disciples were even competitive with each other, like James and John, the sons of Zebedee, vying for future positions on either side of Jesus in the Kingdom of heaven; they were loyal to an extent, but then Peter, who had vowed complete allegiance to Jesus, denied Him three times, and the others pretty much tucked their tails between their legs and ran from Jesus in His final hour on this earth. Yes, they were His followers, but they were not yet sanctified. They were not holy and whole. They were not filled with fruit. They needed the Holy Spirit, just as you and I and all the other followers of Jesus need Him."

•   •   •

With Scripture taking on a whole new dimension for me, coming to life off the pages as Pastor Hearn taught me, I began piecing together the old and familiar with my new, growing understanding. As the days, weeks, and then months progressed, he would bring me books and tapes of testimonies and sermons given by inspirational speakers at Indian Springs Holiness Campmeeting as well as from the faculty at Asbury College and Seminary.

I was so encouraged by amazing people of God like Dr. Dennis Kinlaw, who would eventually become my mentor and dear friend. At the time, he was president of Asbury College in Wilmore, Kentucky. A scholar and a saint, Dr. Kinlaw's story gave me such hope because his heart had searched everywhere for Jesus, just like mine. I devoured the books on the doctrine of Holiness by Salvationist Samuel Brengle and read all the little sermonette books by Dr. John R. Church. I was hungry, and Jesus was feeding me in lots of different ways.

Loving the hymns of our faith and growing up singing my heart out, I started to apply their timeless truths to what Pastor Hearn had been instructing me. Remembering the words to the third verse of *The Old Rugged Cross*, their meaning finally hit home in my heart.

In the old rugged cross, stained with blood so divine,
a wondrous beauty I see;

For 'twas on that old cross Jesus suffered and died,
to pardon and sanctify me.

Oh, my goodness! There it was in black and white: to pardon AND sanctify me!

Then I was reminded of another classic hymn, *Rock of Ages*, with one particular line from the first verse standing out:

Be of sin the double cure, save from wrath and make
me pure.

Wow, there it was again, the fraternal twin concepts of salvation and sanctification: *save from wrath* AND *make me pure.* I began to see how much I needed both.

•   •   •

Sharing my exciting revelation with Pastor Hearn, he revealed more insights from Scripture about the disciples waiting for the same thing I was so hungry to receive, the Holy Spirit. When Jesus appeared to them after the Resurrection, showing them his pierced hands and feet so they would believe who He was, He told them, *"Behold, I send the Promise of My Father upon you; but tarry in the city of Jerusalem until you are endued with power from on high"* (Luke 24:49, NKJV). With that promise of the Holy Spirit, they were filled with joy, praising and blessing God.

Returning to Jerusalem from the Mount of Olives, the disciples continued in prayer and supplication with one accord, celebrating the Feast of Pentecost with other followers of Jesus. Suddenly, like the rushing of a mighty wind, the house where they were staying was filled with tongues as of fire, and they were all filled with the Holy Spirit and with power to do the same things Jesus had said they would do. That was the Spirit of Jesus that Pastor Hearn had spoken of, the love and joy and peace that invaded their lives as they waited and longed for Him with all their hearts.

Now that I saw all these loose threads of Scripture coming together into a unified whole, I could just about see myself right along with them, being filled with the Holy Spirit and with power, receiving that love that I wanted so, so much.

Sensing that, Pastor Hearn said to me, "Joy, when you want Jesus more than anything else in the whole, wide world, that's when it will happen."

~

When You said, "Seek My face," my heart said to You, "Your face, Lord, I will seek." PSALM 27:8, NKJV

"COME AND SEE!"
PART THREE

And you will seek Me and find Me, when you search
for Me with all your heart.   JEREMIAH 29:13, NKJV

HAVING FINALLY BEGUN to grasp the difference between salvation and sanctification, realizing I was saved but not yet set apart, I was still more than a little shocked when Pastor Hearn walked into our living room one day with a *Eureka*-moment expression on his face.

"Joy, I know what your problem is—you're double minded! God's Word tells us in James 1:8, *a double-minded man is unstable in all his ways.* What that means is you're wishy-washy, up and down, blowing hot and cold. You've got just enough of Jesus to make you miserable!"

Well, if I hadn't grown to trust and admire this man as much as I did, I might really have taken offense at his assessment. But it rang true in my heart. In fact, on the day we'd first met months before, I'd even admitted to him I was miserable. So yes, I guess he was right, but I sure didn't want to stay in my state of misery.

Seeing the stricken look on my pale face as I lay on the floor, he gazed gently at me, just as I would imagine Jesus would do, not with condemnation but with the loving conviction that leads to a change of heart. Continuing to explain myself to me, he said, "Joy, you've got one foot over here with Jesus, but your other foot is in the world. 1 John 2:15 says, *Love not the world, nor the things that are in the world.* You're straddling the fence, and that's why it's so painful."

Being a dairy farm girl, I used to have to go into the back pasture to get the cows to be milked, so this "straddling the fence" spoke very graphically to me. I'd have to climb over and around barbed-wire fences that would tear my legs to shreds, which would hurt like crazy. But this spiritual fence-straddling hurt even more.

With that admission, I fully realized how much I wanted to give Jesus everything.

"Please help me, Pastor! How do I do this?" I asked in desperation.

"You surrender everything to Jesus and trust Him to help you," he answered.

"But that's the problem! I don't know how to have faith!" I cried in frustration.

It was then that those words to *I Surrender All* began to come to life for me. I realized I had not given Jesus everything. Before I was paralyzed, I still liked to decide who I would date, how I'd spend my money, what kind of career I would have. Now, unable to move, I no longer had these choices to make, except in my heart. Would I choose now to surrender my life, this broken, immovable body, and whatever future I might have to Jesus?

Pastor Hearn reminded me of I Thessalonians 5:24, a passage we had discussed before: *He who calls you is faithful, who also will do it.* Encouraging me to remember God's promise in that verse, he said, "God is the one who is calling you, and only He can do the work." While I wanted more than anything for him to spell out the steps I needed to take, I knew he was right. He left me then, knowing Jesus was in that room, waiting to fulfill His promise.

With my parents and brother asleep in their rooms on that muggy July night, all the windows open to allow for a whisper of a breeze to stir the heavy air, I shared my dilemma with Jesus, the only one who could solve it.

"Jesus, I don't know how to have faith."

With our cows so near I could hear the sticky-slurpy chewing of their cud, accompanied by the percussive chirps of the crickets, I listened closely for His voice.

Just as Jesus often spoke to His followers in parables, I sensed He was speaking to me right then by reminding me of two life illustrations about trust, both of which had taken place during my early teen years. The first was when I was 15 and had just gotten my learner's permit to drive a car. In Georgia, you're allowed to drive at that age if a parent is in the car with you, so my daddy would sit in the passenger seat as I took the wheel. Now, I knew how trustworthy he was because he had always looked out for my best interests, so when we came to a crossroads out there in the country, he would always say, "Joy, it's clear on the right. You can go," knowing I had already looked to the left. I never questioned whether he was right; I just knew he would be because I trusted his character.

The second example that came to mind was when I was working as a lifeguard at the local swimming pool. I loved teaching little kids to dog paddle, hold their breath, blow bubbles, learn to kick. But the highlight of teaching swimming was the final day when parents and grandparents were invited to witness what their sweet ones had learned. As these squirmy, suntanned little bodies lined up at the diving board in response to my instruction, their excited faces reflected a gleeful kind of terror, the same kind you get before riding a rollercoaster. Despite the fact that the diving board was only about a meter above the water, to them it was like jumping from the moon into the ocean.

As each child would advance toward the end of the board, some would bravely jump right in, but most would waver in a dance of indecision, peering at the water with panicked fascination. *Should I . . . or should I not?* Advance and retreat. Back and forth.

Finally, I would shout up to them, "Jump! I promise I'll catch you! You can trust me!" All they needed to do was take a step and do their part, and I would do mine.

"Joy, just take one step and jump!" The unmistakable voice of Jesus spoke right then and there to me. I could trust Him.

•   •   •

I couldn't wait for Pastor Hearn to arrive the next morning. Beaming from the inside out, I announced, "I'm ready. I want Jesus more than absolutely anything in the world." As we prayed, I was suddenly set free from striving and needing to prove myself, from doubt, anger and resentment. I was free of double mindedness and the trappings of this world. I was being filled with a love unlike any I had ever known, just as Pastor Hearn had tried to describe. This was the fruit of the Spirit of Jesus! I had the Holy Spirit alive and moving in me!

No longer straddling the fence with one foot in and one foot out, it was as if I had been given a brand-new heart, free of every grudge and offense. I wanted others, even those who had hurt me, to have even more of Jesus than I did! My heart was bouncing off the walls with the joyous intensity of this revelation. I wanted to leap up and dance a jig, but even though I still couldn't move, it didn't matter so much because it was well with my soul. Even if I had to lay on that pallet for a hundred years, my soul was rejoicing in my Savior!

After we prayed, I felt so clean and fresh, although nothing unusual had transpired in a physical sense. Wanting more than anything for my heart change to be permanent and not something that would fade, I mentioned to Pastor Hearn that I had read books like *Dark Night of the Soul* by St. John of the Cross, as well as some of the mystical works of Madame Jeanne Guyon, describing the painful struggles they had each encountered, even after their radical surrender to Jesus.

"Pastor, I don't want that to happen to me. How do I keep this?" I asked.

He smiled big and said, "It's easy, Joy! So easy that many miss it. It's all in your personal quiet time and daily devotions. Read your Bible and pray every single day, because that's how God talks to you. You'll be able to see His Word in a new way every day!"

Suggesting I read the little book of I John towards the end of the New Testament, he said, "I want you to read this over and over, until it's real and sealed in your heart."

Knowing to be obedient, I did exactly as he suggested. With my new heart, these words became love letters from

Jesus to me, telling me exactly what I needed to know about this fruit called love. I ate and ate, the juice of the Word dripping into my heart with a sweetness even better than any Georgia peach.

Beloved, let us love one another, for love is of God; and everyone who loves is born of God and knows God. He who does not love does not know God, for God is love. In this the love of God was manifested toward us, that God has sent His only begotten Son into the world, that we might live through Him. In this is love, not that we loved God, but that He loved us and sent His Son to be the propitiation for our sins. Beloved, if God so loved us, we also ought to love one another (I John 4:7-11, NKJV).

Love has been perfected among us in this: that we may have boldness in the day of judgment; because as He is, so are we in this world. There is no fear in love, but perfect love casts out fear, because fear involves torment. But he who fears has not been made perfect in love. We love Him because He first loved us (I John 4:17-19, NKJV).

This is He who came by water and blood—Jesus Christ; not only by water, but by water and blood. And it is the Spirit who bears witness, because the Spirit is truth. For there are three that bear witness in heaven: the Father, the Word, and the Holy Spirit; and these three are one. And there are three that bear witness on earth: the Spirit, the water, and the blood; and these three agree as one (I John 5:6-8, NKJV).

This was what I had been looking for all along, but my heart couldn't receive it because I had not yet fully surrendered. Having sought Jesus for years, searching for Him all the way from a little country church to a big-city seminary, I finally found Him lying flat on my back on the floor. I gave all I had to Him, and He gave me all I would ever need. Himself.

~

Now this is the confidence that we have in Him, that if we ask anything according to His will, He hears us. And if we know that He hears us, whatever we ask, we know that we have the petitions that we have asked of Him.   I JOHN 5:14-15, NKJV

"COME AND SEE!"
PART FOUR

Jesus said to him, "Rise, take up your bed and walk."
And immediately the man was made well, took up
his bed, and walked. JOHN 5:8-9, NKJV

STILL JUBILANT IN THE AFTERGLOW of my spiritual
heart transplant, I was eager to share my story with anyone
who cared to listen. Having been isolated for the previous
eighteen months, I wanted desperately to venture outside
the walls of our little farmhouse and tell others how Jesus
had changed my heart.

Every summer in the county where we lived in rural
Georgia, there were Methodist camp meetings that had
taken place annually for at least 150 years. With rustic,
open-air structures set in the fragrant, piney woods, these
revival meetings would attract young and old from miles
around. My family always went, but I hadn't been able to
go the previous year because of my paralysis.

One day shortly after my radical change of heart, my
parents came into the living room with the local newspaper. "Joy, look at this! See if you know anybody that's
speaking at the camp meeting next week." As they held
the paper so I could see an article with pictures of the
featured speakers, I recognized a classmate from my

brief stint at the seminary who would serve as the camp youth director.

"Hey, I know this guy! He was at the seminary with me and we talked about how we were both struggling with what holiness was all about. I would really like to see him and his wife, to tell them all about how Jesus has changed my heart," I said. My parents knew it was excruciatingly painful for me to be moved, but they suggested perhaps they could lay me in the back seat of the car and take me to the meeting with them. Excited at the prospect of sharing my good news with these friends, I agreed.

Although the deeply-rutted dirt roads made me grit my teeth to endure the pain, I was overjoyed when we arrived at the camp, sensing I was supposed to be there. Laying me and my pallet carefully on the cement porch slab, my parents went off to greet their friends as mine came over and welcomed me back. With my brain and my mouth in serious overdrive, I began to share how Jesus had poured out His love on me through the Holy Spirit.

"Wow, Joy—that's incredible!" said my friends from the seminary. Just then, a car pulled up and an older gentleman emerged, someone I recognized from his picture in the newspaper article my parents had shown me. I knew he was an evangelist named Tom Barrett from south Georgia and was connected somehow to Asbury Seminary in Kentucky, as well as with Indian Springs Holiness Camp Meeting. Both of these would prove to be incredibly influential in my life.

Coming over to where I was lying on the cement, he peered down at me and said rhetorically, "You're not lying there for the fun of it, are you?" Before I could even say a thing, my seminary friend jumped in and told him all about my accident. Thinking this man would probably respond with polite sympathy just like everyone else, I had no expectation of anything different. Most people who met me after the accident would say, "Oh, I'm so sorry. I'll be praying for you." But no one seemed to have any hope that I could be healed, and no one had actually offered to pray for me in person.

"Have you ever asked God to heal you?" asked Rev. Barrett. Caught completely off guard, I had to take a moment to even think of a response. My inner self was saying, "Don't you understand that I just pray for enough relief from pain to be able to fall asleep every night?" I didn't really think healing was an option for me.

Without waiting for a response, Rev. Barrett continued, "Honey, I don't claim to understand healing. I don't know why some are healed and some are not; why we sometimes go to church and pray for someone to be healed, and then they die the same week. But I do know that everywhere in the gospels where it says they brought people to Jesus, He healed them. The Bible says in Hebrews 13:8, *Jesus Christ is the same yesterday, and today, and forever.* It also tells us in James 5:14 to call on the elders to pray. I just want you to know I'm willing to ask Jesus for you to be healed."

"Yes, sir, I'd like you to pray for me. But I don't have much expectation."

"Well, young lady, Jesus says in Matthew 18:19, *'If two of you agree on earth concerning anything that they ask, it will be done for them by My Father in heaven.'*

Before I pray, I want to know what you can agree with me on. Would you agree with me that God could heal you in six months?"

"Yes, sir. But six months is a long way off, and I know that the people I know would not give God the credit if He did heal me because they'd probably say I just got better gradually, or maybe that I'd had a special surgery. I want people to know the same Jesus I know, the Jesus who radically healed my heart two weeks ago. I don't want any human being to get the credit for what God does because no one is good but God. I want Him to get all the glory!"

Now I want to make clear that I firmly believe God uses the gifts He has given doctors and nurses and pharmacologists and other medical personnel to bring healing to His children. I believe most people are healed gradually in that way. Instantaneous healing, at least in the times in which we live, is unusual.

"So, Joy, could you agree with me that God could heal you right now?" he asked.

Bursting into tears, I cried, "No, sir. I can't. I'm in so much pain and I can't even move. The doctors say I'll never move again. I can't imagine even sitting up in a chair, much less walking or running. I'll never be able to walk down the aisle to get married or have babies!" I was completely undone.

Persisting gently but firmly, Rev. Barrett said, "I don't mean to be flippant, Joy. But tell me this: Before two weeks ago, could you ever have imagined feeling the kind of love, joy, and peace God gave you when He sanctified you and filled you with His Spirit?"

Only God could have led him to say that, because it suddenly took my mind off myself and refocused it soundly on Jesus. As I recaptured the glory of the miracle He had done on my heart two weeks before, I realized it was the greatest thing I could ever imagine, even more for me than the miraculous parting of the Red Sea, because Jesus had made my heart totally clean and filled it with His love.

Answering Rev. Barrett's question, I said, "That was the greatest miracle I could even imagine, having my heart become clean like that. If God could do that for me, I know He can do anything."

Without asking my permission, brother Tom launched into a conversation with God, so simple and straight-forward, no flowery language, no *Thee's* and *Thou's*. I don't remember specifically the words he used until he said this: "Father, because of Matthew 18:19, I agree with Joy that it is DONE!"

With those words, everything was suddenly different, as if I had gone absolutely numb. Feeling like I must have fallen asleep, I was aware of the conspicuous absence of pain. I thought, *It's so wonderful to not hurt! I hope nobody wakes me up because I could stay like this forever!*

But brother Tom was very present and asked, "Joy, did anything happen?"

"I don't know," I said very tentatively, reluctant to ver-balize my thoughts.

"Well, can you move anything?" he persisted.

Not stopping to see if I could even wiggle my toes, I shot up off the ground like a rocket. Thrusting my arms up and my legs out, I did jumping jacks, I ran in place, I leaned backwards, performing a back bend like a gymnast—everything I used to do! It was as if I had never been paralyzed. There was absolutely not even any muscle atrophy, something that defies the laws of medical science.

Just a few hours after I leapt off the ground, praising God like the paralyzed beggar in Acts 3, God gave me another miracle. My monthly period, which had been dormant for the past 18 months, suddenly started. At the time, I was so preoccupied with just being able to move again that I didn't quite wrap around the fact that the dreams I thought had died, thoughts of a husband and children, might still come true. God had truly answered every single prayer.

The following morning, which was a Sunday, I got up, put on my running shoes, and ran two miles before going to church. I was so, so exhilarated at the thought of sharing my great news with everyone. But even before church, I knew I'd have another opportunity literally coming down the road any minute!

Every day of my young life, for as far back as I could remember, a giant tanker truck would come to our dairy farm to pick up the milk. Reliable as clockwork, the Atlanta Dairies company would send Mr. Joe, our milkman, every 24 hours to collect our cows' daily offerings. My parents milked twice daily, both in the mornings and in the evenings, to fill a five-hundred-gallon tank that needed to be emptied without fail every day.

Rumbling down our country road early every morning, Mr. Joe's truck could be heard a mile away as he downshifted after leaving the highway. He would drive directly to the barn, taking the milk's temperature to ensure it was cooled enough to be piped into the tanker. Checking for butterfat to make sure there was no bitterweed in the milk, Mr. Joe would then pump it through a huge hose, like that on a fire truck, hooked through an opening in the barn wall right into his truck.

Since I had known Mr. Joe all my life, he was like part of our family. As a little girl, I'd be out with my parents early every morning as they cleaned the barn and Mr. Joe collected the milk, a process that took about 45 minutes. Since he had to wait for the milk to be pumped through the hose into his truck, Mr. Joe would always take time to be my friend, singing songs with me and quoting Bible verses. He made me feel so valued, and when I became paralyzed, it hurt his heart.

During the year and a half when I was lying immobile on my pallet in the living room, I would listen for Mr. Joe's truck every morning, able to distinguish its motor from the school bus that came around the same time. He would always honk his horn on the way down to the barn, and if he had time, he would stop his truck in front of our house, run up to the screen door, and holler, "Hey, girl! How ya' doin' today?"

So, on this most memorable Sunday morning, I just couldn't wait to tell Mr. Joe that Jesus had healed me. Timing my run so I would be on the stretch of road where I could see him round the bend about a third of a mile ahead of me, I got ready to meet the truck. But when Mr. Joe turned into the curve and saw me running, the incredulous expression on his face looked as if he had seen a ghost.

Suddenly fearful for his life, I shouted out loud, "Protect him, Jesus, or he's going to jackknife and die!" The front end of the trailer was actually veering toward the ditch, but Jesus stopped it just in time.

Quickly climbing up the steep ladder to the cab, I saw with great relief that he was okay. "Mr. Joe!" I shouted through the window, "Jesus healed me last night!" With tears streaming down his weathered face, my old friend said, "Well, I knew you were a Christian. And the Bible says if you just ask, you will be healed." Now I want to interject that this isn't exactly what the Bible says, but he thought it was. Anyhow, before I had time to respond, Mr. Joe looked down with shame and said, "Of course, I'm not a Christian."

Completely shocked, I looked at him and said, "Mr. Joe, are you kidding me? How can you say that? You know as much Scripture as anybody I know!"

"No," he said. "I got married before the war. And when I was fighting overseas, I did some things I never should have done. There's just no way God can forgive me."

"Oh, Mr. Joe! That's not true. Of course, He can forgive you!"

Having just experienced my own radical change of heart through complete surrender to Jesus' cleansing blood, I began to share with my lifelong friend what it means to be forgiven and made holy and whole. Explaining as best I could that all Jesus asks is for us to confess our sins, repent of our old ways, and believe in Him, Mr. Joe surrendered his life to Jesus and accepted the forgiveness He paid for on the cross.

Feeling as if Mr. Joe and I had just had church together, I couldn't wait to see what would happen when I entered the church building I thought I'd never walk into again.

Since everyone in our little town knew me and the circumstances of my accident, those at church that day could see my healing was authentic. One day I had been lying flat on a pallet on the floor; the next I was walking and leaping and praising God! Seven days later, I would drive to the next county and run a 10K race, 6.2 miles. Just as in Acts 3:10 after the paralytic is healed, the people were all filled with wonder and amazement at what God had done.

*   *   *

Wanting to honor those who had devoted so much of themselves to me for the duration of my paralysis, I couldn't wait to tell Pastor and Mrs. Hearn what Jesus had done. Having been instrumental in the process of teaching me about sanctification and the second work of grace by the power of the Holy Spirit, they deserved to not only hear but see the fruit of their prayers. Knowing they would be attending Indian Springs Holiness Campmeeting at that time, I decided to drive to south Georgia the Monday after I was healed.

With Indian Springs being the largest camp meeting in the South, and one of the largest in the country, I knew it might be a challenge to find the Hearns in the midst of thousands of other people. In an era long before cell phones were in use, I relied on good, old-fashioned word of mouth to find them. Directed to their cabin, I decided to literally run in and surprise them.

Their jaws dropping open in amazement, the Hearns were momentarily speechless. But as they recognized that Jesus had healed me physically, just as He had touched my heart and healed my soul, we began to thank and praise God together for His miraculous work in my life.

Immediately, Pastor Hearn wanted to introduce me to seemingly everyone at the camp. With three worship services and an adult Bible study every day over a ten-day period, in addition to early morning prayer meetings and other activities, this meant I was in for a lot of introductions! So grateful to be in this place that had influenced and impacted my life already through the recorded sermons he had shared with me, I sensed I was meeting people who would become like family to me.

* * *

Physical healing was one of the primary means Jesus used in biblical times to convey the love of God to His children because it immediately captured their attention.

I am forever grateful to be able to stand on my two feet and witness to people about the healing power of Jesus. But for me, the most important thing God did was to transform my heart. Every one of us needs a heart transplant, the heart of Jesus, to fill us with a love unlike any other.

My heart's desire is for all God's children to be made holy and whole, to receive all the love He has to give.

~

For this reason I bow my knees to the Father of our Lord Jesus Christ, from whom the whole family in heaven and earth is named, that He would grant you, according to the riches of His glory, to be strengthened with might through His Spirit in the inner man, that Christ may dwell in your hearts through faith; that you, being rooted and grounded in love, may be able to comprehend with all the saints what is the width and length and depth and height— to know the love of Christ which passes knowledge; that you may be filled with all the fullness of God. Now to Him who is able to do exceedingly abundantly above all that we ask or think according to the power that works in us, to Him be glory in the church by Christ Jesus to all generations, forever and ever. Amen.   EPHESIANS 3:14-21, NKJV

ANSWERING THE CALL

ANSWERING THE CALL
PART ONE

And these words which I command you today shall be in your heart. You shall teach them diligently to your children and shall talk of them when you sit in your house, when you walk by the way, when you lie down, and when you rise up. You shall bind them as a sign on your hand, and they shall be as frontlets between your eyes. You shall write them on the doorposts of your house and on your gates.

DEUTERONOMY 6:6-9, NKJV

I GREW UP IN A PRIVILEGED HOME, a truly rich home. Rich in mercy, rich in love, rich in the ways of God. Our wealth was not of this world, but it was of the kind that will never fade or perish. My parents were humble, honest, hard-working people who loved the Lord with all their heart, loved their neighbors as themselves, and raised my brother and me to walk in His ways.

Brought up on a dairy farm in northwest Georgia, honesty and integrity were instilled in me from the cradle. God first, family second—and everything else would fall into place. Dishonesty, laziness, and selfishness were not in our family's vocabulary. My parents epitomized sacrificial lives of service, putting others before themselves.

My father, Edward Smith, was just 19 years old when he enlisted in the United States Army. From the same hometown as my mother, Marie Bartlett, he was good friends with her three older brothers, Ed, Newt, and Louis. But with Marie being just a little squirt of 12, my daddy just thought of her as his buddies' kid sister.

With just one month left to serve in the military before discharge, his world was rocked with the shocking news of the bombing of Pearl Harbor on December 7, 1941. Thrust into World War II without warning, he was placed in Company D of the 121st Infantry Division, sent to Germany and then France. Involved in some of the most ferocious, strategic battles of the war, including the Battle of the Bulge and the Normandy Invasion, it was truly a miracle he survived.

A couple of years ago, a few years after my father's death, I had the opportunity to visit Normandy while en route to a conference in Belgium. Taking a train to the northwestern region of France. I visited Omaha Beach and Utah Beach, where my daddy had served. As I stood on the sand where his division had landed, I was gripped with awe, wondering how any of these brave soldiers had survived. Daddy had told us how he had swum through the turbulent waters, strewn with body parts, in the midst of gunfire from every angle. Many of his buddies never made it to the beach, sacrificing their lives to ensure our freedom. They were true heroes.

Blessedly, with the Allied victory, Edward Smith was able to return to his roots in Georgia. Having sent all his Army paychecks—17 dollars each month—back to his father for safekeeping during the war, he used that money to purchase the land that would eventually become our farm. In the meantime, he renewed his friendship with the Bartlett brothers, and in the process, discovered their little sister Marie had transformed into a raving beauty. A romantic courtship ensued, and they were married on November 22, 1947.

Momma was working at the Bell South telephone company as she and Daddy began building up the farm, adding two large chicken houses in addition to the dairy barn. When the farm was established enough to provide a viable income, she quit working at the phone company and devoted her time and energy to our family and the farm.

I always loved it when people would say, "Joy, you look just like your mother!" in my opinion not only was she beautiful in appearance, she looked more like Jesus than anyone I've ever met. Never conscious of her many attributes, she was like the virtuous woman described in Proverbs 31. I wanted to be just like her. My daddy was the perfect complement to her, a protective, caring man who loved unconditionally. How incredibly blessed I was to be raised by them. Wes and I named our children Hannah Marie, for the biblical Hannah and my mother, Marie, and Caleb Edward, for Caleb in the Bible and Edward, my father.

Some of my earliest memories are of my mother taking me along with her to visit neighbors who were less fortunate than we were, many of them uneducated and living without basic necessities like running water. Sometimes she would quietly deposit a gift of homecooked food or some clothing items on their doorstep rather than cause them to feel shame or embarrassment at receiving charity. My parents believed and practiced what Jesus said in Matthew 6:3, *"But when you give to the needy, do not let your left hand know what your right hand is doing"* (NIV).

Likewise, their prayer lives modeled Jesus' teaching in that same passage from the Sermon on the Mount. *"When you pray, go into your room, close the door and pray to your Father, who is unseen. Then your Father, who sees what is done in secret, will reward you"* (Matthew 6:6, NIV). Up with the roosters well before dawn, their first call was to honor Jesus before all else.

Momma and Daddy would then head out from our farmhouse to milk the 60 or 70 Holsteins I sometimes helped herd into the barn. Actually, it was our loyal Border Collie, Shep, who really did most of the work, but I was Shep's encourager. After milking, the lots had to be cleaned, fences repaired, and thousands of chickens fed. Then there was the bush hogging (cutting grass and clearing the land), raking, and baling hay the cows would need for food in the winter. After all that, the same process would be repeated in the afternoons around 4 o'clock, an endless loop that never varied. But with God first, there always seemed to be time for family, friends, neighbors, and church and school activities.

Oh, how I loved those days on the farm, especially in the summertime when school was out. Although I did have a little doll family I tended to like most little girls, my real passion was for the outdoors. Getting together with friends and cousins, we would challenge each other to see who could climb the highest tree, run the fastest race, catch the biggest fish, gather the most lightning bugs. We'd make mud pies and take mud baths, and then gleefully splash in the creek to wash away the evidence.

Attending the same small country school from first grade through high school, Mt. Zion became like an extension of my family. Always there for one another, the students and their families, teachers, coaches, and club leaders would unfailingly provide support in both good times and bad. Not only did I receive an excellent education, but I learned how to be genuine, unpretentious, and to care as much for others as myself.

There was something so comforting, so reassuring, in the predictability of our relentlessly steady routine. I saw how God always provided everything we truly needed as we trusted in Him and honored His ways. We were taught to be frugal, sometimes washing our hair with bar soap instead of shampoo, or using laundry detergent to wash the dishes, but we were also taught to be generous in sharing with others. My parents demonstrated unconditional love with godly discipline and character, always striving to tell the truth and live humble lives of service to others.

I believe many of the life lessons and principles I learned from my parents on the farm have translated into my calling as a missionary. With cows, goats, and chickens as my constant companions, I never had to think twice about sleeping in cow-manure huts, eating goat guts, or being chased by squawking chickens or any other critters, for that matter. I was being trained in cultural relevance long before I'd ever even heard the term.

Even today, when people comment on the work I do on the mission field, I tell them I am simply an extension of those who have gone before me and those who pray for me. There are many times when I'm traveling in faraway places that I wonder whose prayers made it possible for me to be there. I wonder if it might have been a great-grandparent I never met who prayed for their offspring to produce godliness and righteousness in their children and the generations to follow. I wonder if it could have been the prayers of my parents when I was still floating around in my mother's womb. Or maybe it was my loving grandparents, or aunts and uncles, praying for me as I was growing up.

Heaven holds the answers to all these questions. But without a doubt, I humbly acknowledge that anything I do for the kingdom of our Lord Jesus Christ is the result of the intercession of others. I pray my own legacy to Hannah and Caleb will continue what was so lovingly given to me.

~

The secret things belong to the Lord our God, but those things which are revealed belong to us and to our children forever, that we may do all the words of this law.   DEUTERONOMY 29:29, NKJV

ANSWERING THE CALL
PART TWO

Trust in the Lord with all your heart, and lean
not on your own understanding. In all your ways
acknowledge Him, and He shall direct your paths.

PROVERBS 3:5-6, NKJV

FILLED WITH HOLY ZEAL after Jesus healed me of eighteen months of paralysis, I felt like the man in Acts 3:9-10, walking and leaping and praising God! Because all my hometown folks had known I was lying flat on my back, unable to move, they also understood it was only the Lord who could have brought about such a miracle. Just as with those surrounding the formerly lame beggar at the Beautiful Gate of the temple, everyone was filled with awe and wonder at what Jesus had done for me.

As news spread quickly throughout our little community in northwest Georgia and then in ever-widening circles, opportunities came for me to share my testimony in churches. Knowing the privilege I was being given to share Jesus with so many others, I decided to postpone my education by a semester in order to accept these speaking invitations. Sunday mornings and evenings, as well as Wednesday evenings throughout that fall season, were dedicated to telling the good news about Jesus to everyone who had ears to hear and eyes to see.

Having been accepted at Asbury Seminary, I was so excited to actually go to Wilmore, Kentucky, to learn at the same place where so many of my spiritual mentors had studied. From the time I received Jesus in my heart at church camp when I was 12, to being mentored by Rev. Hearn in matters of holiness, to receiving healing when brother Tom Barrett prayed for me, I had seen the thread of Asbury Seminary woven into the tapestry of my life. And now I would experience it firsthand, getting to sit under godly professors who had already influenced me through the testimonies I had heard and read.

While the semester at Asbury actually began in February, they offered an intensive January term with just one class that equaled a semester's worth of credit. I had to pinch myself when my parents dropped me off at the dorm on campus, just to make sure I wasn't dreaming. Soaking up the atmosphere of loving truth surrounding me at every turn, the month of January flew by as if it were a day. It was already time for the short break before classes would resume in February, and I realized I needed to find a ride back home to Georgia.

In those pre-internet days, the typical means of communication was to pin a note to various campus bulletin boards, asking if anyone would be driving to various states and cities. Since I hadn't yet met anyone else from Georgia, I tried that method but got no response. Married couples generally lived in campus housing and wouldn't be traveling, so I needed to find a single person who would be going my way.

One of my new friends in the dorm, Rindi, was a missionary kid from Africa, very resourceful and always willing to help. Telling her I needed to find a ride back home for the break, she paused to think a moment.

"You know, Joy, there's a single guy who was in a class I took who's from Georgia. Maybe he knows someone who is going home for the break." Since Rindi worked in the library, she told me where he usually sat to study, so I marched right up those stairs and, sure enough, found the one she had described.

Seeing this good-looking guy sporting an Atlanta Braves baseball cap, just idly flipping through a magazine, I went over and whispered, "Excuse me, are you Wes Griffin?"

"Yes," he said.

"Well, my name is Joy Smith and my friend Rindi told me you're from Georgia. I'm trying to find a ride back there at the break time. Do you know anyone who's going that way?"

"You know, I'm going—and I'd be glad to give you a ride. I'll pick you up at your dorm at 8 this Saturday morning."

Since we had never really had a conversation other than the 30 seconds it took to arrange my ride, I wasn't sure where all of this might be headed. True to his word, Wes picked me up in front of my dorm early that Saturday morning, and when I got in his car, he immediately said, "So, tell me your testimony. Why did you come to Asbury?"

Since the greatest event of my life had just happened six months earlier, we covered many miles with that story.

Like others who had heard what Jesus did, both in healing my body and revealing the Holy Spirit to me, Wes listened with rapt attention, maybe even a bit more attentively than most. He seemed to really identify with what I was saying and was eager to hear more. Just two or three hours into that drive, I was thinking, *This is the kind of guy I want to marry someday!*

Taking the focus off me and my meandering thoughts, I said, "Now it's your turn. Tell me about you, Wes." So we covered lots more territory as he shared his family background, aspirations, hopes and dreams for the future. I would not know until quite some time later that Wes had been thinking the same thought as I during our conversation, *This is the kind of girl I want to marry someday.* In fact, we now have a special marker of that trip, a bridge on I-75 between Kentucky and Tennessee, where we always kiss as a reminder of how God brought us together.

Since neither one of us was ready for a serious romantic relationship, we just became good buddies and prayer partners throughout our time together at Asbury. Since Wes was a year ahead of me, we didn't share any classes, but would arrange to meet at breaks to talk and pray together. By the time he graduated, we were the best of friends and I knew I would really miss having him nearby on campus. He was ordained into ministry that summer and accepted a pastoral call to a little church about an hour outside of Atlanta.

Just before I was to return to Asbury that August for my final year, Wes asked if I would come to the church he was pastoring to hear him preach one Sunday morning. I was excited to see my good friend again and listen to what the Lord had to say through him, and was not dis-appointed. That evening, I went with him as he led the youth group, and then he suggested we drive a few miles to a larger church in the area with an evening service.

Sitting together near the back of the church, I didn't want the evening to end. As the service came to a close and the pastor invited people to come to the altar for prayer, Wes asked if I would like to do that with him. Nodding my agreement, we got up and made our way to the aisle, when he suddenly reached out and took my hand. Surprised but pleased, I tried hard to focus as we reached the front and knelt together at the altar.

"Lord Jesus," Wes prayed, "We just want to offer our relationship to you. If it's not of you, we don't want it . . . ."

Trying my best to catch a glimpse of his face through my peripheral vision, I thought, *He's thinking what I'm thinking!* Reminded of our very first conversation in the car, I couldn't wait to see what would come next. But then they flipped the lights on in the sanctuary to signify the end of the service and the beginning of Sunday dinner. So, that was that. With people surrounding us, the moment evaporated and nothing more was said.

I had arranged to spend the night with some girls I knew in that little town, but before we parted, Wes said, "Can you maybe come by the parsonage tomorrow morning before you drive back?" I thought that sounded like a good idea, so we agreed on a time and I appeared on his doorstep early Monday morning.

Inviting me into the living room of the simple little house the church provided for their pastor, I sat down on the couch and he joined me. After we talked a bit, Wes gently put his arm around my shoulders and said, "Well, Joy, I guess you know I've fallen really hard and fast for you." All I could say was, "Well, I guess you know it's the same for me."

Just as we were in the middle of our first kiss, there was an abrupt, loud knock on the front door. Grimacing and groaning, he got up to see who it was. Lo and behold, the exterminator had come to do away with the bugs. What a way to extinguish our first kiss!

Oblivious to any romance in the room, the bug man proceeded to thoroughly spray every baseboard throughout the whole house. When he was done, we could hardly breathe, much less kiss. That would just have to wait. I had to leave to drive back to the seminary.

From then on, we were only able to "date" long distance through frequent phone calls and letters over the next several months. But during the January intensive, Wes asked if he could drive up to see me. As the weather began to deteriorate, he was delayed and didn't reach my dorm until 10 that evening. As absolutely everything in Wilmore was shut down on Sunday nights, when Wes suggested, "Let's go somewhere!" our options were seriously limited.

Making our way through the snowy evening to the administration building, we decided to see if the door to the Haskins-Luce prayer chapel was open. A charming, holy space next to the main chapel, it was blessedly unlocked and we went in. With the moonlight streaming through the stained glass windows, we seized the romantic moment, liplocked in a passionate kiss. Suddenly we were startled out of our wits when the lights abruptly flipped on. This time, it wasn't the bug man at the door.

"Uhhh . . . excuse me, f-f-folks," stammered the older man as he rapidly turned bright red. "I'm with campus security and saw you come in here. Thought maybe you were part of the ministers' conference and might like to have a little light."

"No, thanks," said Wes. "We're just fine the way things are."

The security guard hightailed it out of there and we picked up right where we'd left off.

Without wasting any precious time or even turning on the lights, Wes got down on his knees before God and me and asked if I would be his wife. Without hesitation, I said "YES!" as he presented me with a beautiful engagement ring.

The next six months were spent joyfully planning our wedding as I finished seminary. Graduating in May, I had several weeks at home with my parents to finalize plans before the big event. Since it would be held in my hometown of Carrollton, that meant absolutely everyone we knew would be invited, so it ended up being a huge occasion. Married by the Rev. Howell Hearn, that dear man who had devoted so much of his time to teaching me about holiness during my confinement, I wore the whitest dress with the longest train I could find to celebrate our marriage covenant.

Moving into the parsonage with Wes after our wedding and brief honeymoon, I was excited to join my new husband in shepherding the church. Helping lead the youth group as well as a women's discipleship group, I also played the piano for services while Wes preached. After we served there together for two years, Wes was called to another church in Forsyth, Georgia, about 90 miles away from my hometown.

Learning that we were expecting our first child, everyone in the church was nearly as excited as we were. Deciding it would be reassuring for me to give birth in Carrollton, where I could have our family doctor deliver the baby, I also wanted to be surrounded by my family and circle of close friends. Our beautiful Hannah Marie was brought safely into the world, making us a family of three and transforming our lives. Two years later, while expecting Caleb, I made the same decision. Greeting our baby boy for the first time in the midst of those who knew and loved me best was a slice of heaven on earth.

Our church in Forsyth became like extended family to us as we began raising our children there. Carting Hannah and Caleb to youth group activities, women's meetings, Sunday school classes, and church suppers, I had more eager babysitters than I could count as our little treasures captured the hearts of everyone around them. We understood more than ever what it meant to be part of the family of God.

Now, therefore, you are no longer strangers and foreigners, but fellow citizens with the saints and members of the household of God, having been built on the foundation of the apostles and prophets, Jesus Christ Himself being the chief cornerstone, in whom the whole building, being fitted together, grows into a holy temple in the Lord. EPHESIANS 2:19-21, NKJV

ANSWERING THE CALL
PART THREE

"It is not for you to know times or seasons which the Father has put in His own authority. But you shall receive power when the Holy Spirit has come upon you; and you shall be witnesses to Me in Jerusalem, and in all Judea and Samaria, and to the end of the earth."   ACTS 1:7-8, NKJV

BLISSFULLY CONTENT in my role as a preacher's wife and the mother of two adorable toddlers, I was fully aware of the words penned by King Solomon in Ecclesiastes 3:1, *To everything there is a season, a time for every purpose under heaven* (NKJV). Even as I savored these precious moments of our daily routine, my thoughts would sometimes wander back to seminary days, reflecting on a lifechanging event in the middle of my second year that would influence the rest of my days on earth. Could the Holy Spirit be preparing us for another change of season?

Replaying my middle year at Asbury Seminary, I could viscerally feel the anticipation of one of those "firsts" in life—my very first trip outside the United States. Not only that, but the destination would be India, about as far from my Georgia upbringing as one could get. I was one of a group of twelve, including nine men and three women, who would be earning credit during the January intensive for our course in Christian Missions taught by J.T. Seamands.

Dr. Seamands was, simply put, a legend in his own time. Raised in India as the son of missionary parents, J.T. and his brother David both studied at Asbury College and Seminary, returning there after graduation to serve as their parents had. When J.T. retired from missions in India, he and his wife Ruth moved back to the States, where he became Professor of Christian Missions at Asbury Seminary.

J.T. and Ruth Seamands had a profound influence on my life and preparation for ministry on the mission field. I signed up for every course I could take under Dr. Seamands, and devoured not only his books, but those written by his wife. Ruth Seamands' book, *Missionary Mama*, influenced me long before I was a wife and mother by describing what real life on the mission field entails, both the positive and negative aspects.

Despite Dr. Seamands' efforts to make his students ready for a paradigm shift in culture, absolutely nothing could have prepared us for the sights, sounds, and stench of India. A teeming sea of humanity moving in every conceivable direction, the traffic alone was overwhelming. Add honking horns, shouting, chanting, blaring music, even a funeral procession marching down a major avenue with the deceased lying high up on a bier, and you begin to get the picture. With 623 million people then, and close to 1.4 billion now, there wasn't much wiggle room for anybody.

With an infrastructure lacking in proper waste management, sewers, toilet facilities, and clean water, the result is air reeking so thick you can almost taste it. Assaulting our senses, the putrid stench of excrement, perspiration, burning waste, stagnant water, and who knows what else caused us to wretch at first. But we were on a mission, and knew God would help us overcome our frail human nature.

Having never been to a foreign country before, much less one in the Third World, I was thankful to have been indoctrinated in some of the cultural customs and taboos. Public displays of affection are not welcome there, nor is it appropriate to wear revealing clothing like shorts or sleeveless shirts. You never touch, offer, or accept anything with the left hand, as it is traditionally expected to be used in lieu of toilet paper. One never points at anything with the index figure, especially something sacred. Shoes are always removed when entering someone's home or a temple.

Traveling far and wide, going to places the Seamands' had served as God multiplied their efforts over the years, we began to realize that, despite poor communication, word always got out that J.T. Seamands was on his way for a visit. Feeling very much like the disciples of Jesus as they watched their Master at work, we also noted the deep humility of our professor whose only desire was to serve. Surprised that people would hover around us and even try to kiss our feet because we were with him, Dr. Seamands would say to them, "No, no—we give all the glory to Jesus. This is all for Him."

An exceptionally tall man, J.T. was also very white-skinned and freckled, as redheads often are. Despite growing up in that country, he looked nothing like the natives. However, I have dark hair and eyes, and sitting in the sun can enhance my resemblance to an Indian woman. Wearing a traditional *sari*, I could just about pass as a native if I didn't open my mouth. But J.T. encouraged his students to dive right in, preaching and teaching, taking part in baptisms and dedications.

This was the first time I had ever experienced working with a translator, along with most of my classmates. Dr. Seamands had coached us in advance to speak slowly, using short sentences. But the most ominous part was when he said, "Be careful with your words, because God's Word is at stake." What he meant was that complex terms are often not able to be readily understood in another language, or some cultural idioms may not make any sense at all. He imbued us with a healthy respect for cultural relevance.

Illustrating this point by sharing a personal experience, Dr. Seamands told us about a time he and Ruth were ministering in a village they hadn't been to before. Since India has over 500 dialects, they soon ran into a bit of a pickle (case in point for avoiding idioms). J.T. was teaching on John 6, where Jesus says, *"I am the bread of life. Whoever comes to Me will never go hungry . . ."* Suddenly the translator was silent. Not understanding the problem, J.T. looked at him quizzically. Then it occurred to J.T. that these people did not have bread in their diet. They didn't even have a word for it.

As he and Ruth put their heads together, it dawned on them that these people ate sweet potatoes as the main form of starch in their diet. So J.T. repeated John 6:35, changing *bread* to *sweet potato*: *"I am the sweet potato of life. Whoever comes to Me will never go hungry . . ."*

As the text took on meaning for them, the people nodded enthusiastically, rejoicing in this Jesus who would feed them so they would never go hungry.

"Did I change the gospel?" our professor asked. "No. I only changed my presentation of the gospel to make it understandable for them." I would never forget that lesson, and would apply it in my own work years later in the Amazon jungle.

Visiting major cities like Bombay (now Mumbai), Calcutta, and Delhi, we soon noted the extreme difference between the haves and the have-nots, all based on the caste system. While there is a common misconception of just four castes, there are actually thousands of them, many of them regional. But the lowest caste, the *untouchables* or *Dalits,* are universally discarded by society as if they were no more valuable than a fly or even dirt. As most of India practices the Hindu religion which teaches reincarnation, they believe touching a member of the lowest caste will defile them. Social ostracism is so strong that marrying into a lower caste will cause estrangement from a family. Converting to Christianity carries the same stigma.

Another group of *untouchables* includes anyone who has leprosy, regardless of caste status. Still a major problem in India, this bacterial disease is not readily transmissible through casual contact like hugging or shaking hands, but carries a huge stigma, as if merely touching a leper would cause you to catch the disease. For that reason, lepers live in colonies far removed from mainstream civilization. Since even family members fear contracting it, they do not come to visit their loved ones. It isn't unusual for them to leave gifts of oranges, bananas, or some other type of fruit five miles outside the leper colony, hoping it will be retrieved by one of the caregivers.

Having never seen anyone with leprosy before, I wasn't sure what to expect. As we entered the colony, I soon saw very graphically that it is a gruesome, flesh-eating disease. The evidence surrounded us, with victims who had lost a nose, an ear, fingers, hands, arms, feet, legs. The compassion of Jesus welled up in me as I saw the shame and fear of rejection on their faces.

Approaching one, I extended my hand and she slowly reached for it, a smile breaking forth on her face. As I walked around, touching some on the head, patting others on the back, tears would come into the deep pools of their eyes. I was just doing what I knew Jesus would do.

After leaving the colony, we came across an old, rail-thin, crippled man by the side of the road. By his side were halves of what appeared to be watermelon, although the red fruit was more the size of a large grapefruit. Apparently, this was how he earned his living.

"Do you like watermelon?" he asked me.

"Well, yes I do," I admitted, although I was glancing skeptically at the maggot-infested slices resting in the dirt at my feet.

"I want to thank you for all you have done for us, and for praying for me. I don't know how to thank you except to give you what I have," he said with sincere emotion.

"Thank you, that's so kind of you!" I answered, as he handed the fruit to me.

But he was staring at me intently, watching to see if I would eat it. A bullet prayer was going up faster than you could blink an eye or swat a fly. *Lord Jesus, please help me to not throw up! Please help me to not feel these maggots crawling in my throat or belly or intestines! Please help me to not get sick!"* And just as He always does, the Lord heard and answered me. I learned the truth of 2 Corinthians 4:7, *But we have this treasure in earthen vessels, that the excellence of the power may be of God and not of us* (NKJV).

With so many opportunities to minister throughout India, we were astonished at how God moved among us, despite our inexperience and amateurish efforts. In one little village, after we prayed for a blind woman, she received her sight. In another, demonic spirits manifested in two men as we were preaching, so we prayed over them and the Holy Spirit brought calm deliverance and freedom in Jesus. Several children were healed of different deformities while we were there. The onlookers were thrilled to learn about Jesus, who heals and sets people free.

As Dr. Seamands led our team, we learned firsthand the importance of dealing with the salvation of souls before administering healing prayer. In a polytheistic culture with thousands of gods and no promise of eternal life, how glorious it was to see the power of the one true God manifested through His healing grace and deliverance from evil!

This trip was transformational for me. Not only was it my introduction to culturally relevant evangelism, it was where I fully began to understand what it is to love like Jesus. To visit great sites like the Taj Mahal, four hours outside Delhi, and then witness half-clothed, starving people eating from garbage dumps right outside the gates was a dichotomy I couldn't quite wrap around. To see millions of people discarded like dirt because they were born to parents who were *untouchable* broke my heart. To know lepers were isolated from the rest of humanity because no one understood the disease that was consuming them was a call to action.

What I really wanted to do was touch the *untouchables* and reach the *unreachables*. Jesus died to give them life, so maybe God was showing me what He wanted me to do with my life. Having committed myself at age 13 to whatever He called me to, wherever He wanted to send me, I needed to know if this was it.

"God," I prayed, "You've got to help me. Otherwise, all I can do is cry because I see need everywhere I look. Please just help me to see as Jesus sees."

Suddenly, I could really relate to Matthew 9:36-38. *But when He saw the multitudes, He was moved with compassion for them, because they were weary and scattered, like sheep having no shepherd. Then He said to His disciples, "The harvest truly is plentiful, but the laborers are few. Therefore pray the Lord of the harvest to send out laborers into His harvest"* (NKJV).

I was willing to be one of those laborers.

~

He has shown you, O mortal, what is good. And what does the Lord require of you? To act justly and to love mercy and to walk humbly with your God.   MICAH 6:8, NIV

MISSION: ESTONIA

MISSION: ESTONIA
PART ONE

How, then, can they call on the one they have not
believed in? And how can they believe in the one of
whom they have not heard? And how can they hear
without someone preaching to them? And how can
they preach unless they are sent? As it is written,
"How beautiful are the feet of those who bring
good news!"   ROMANS 10:14-15, NIV

ONE OF THE GREAT HEROES of our faith that I can't wait
to meet in heaven is William Carey, known as the father
of modern missions. Raised in the Church of England, he
labored as a shoe cobbler, hammering away on heels and
praying for souls. Taking a scrap of leather, he cut a rough
map of the world and hung it on the wall so he could pray
for God's children as he worked.

Having a vision to take the gospel to India, Carey gathered with a small group of friends, describing his call from
God as being like a rescue mission into a deep, dark well.
"I will go down into the pit," he told them, "if you will hold
the ropes." This resulted not only in their agreeing to hold
the ropes through fervent intercession, but in the formation
of what would be known as the Baptist Missionary Society.

I remember hearing a story that really stuck with me as

an illustration underscoring the vital importance of praying Rope Holders in missions work. Written by Rick and Cindy Gray, it was shared at Echo Church in Pleasant Hill, Missouri, on January 9, 2016.

ROPE HOLDERS

Through the streets of a fishing village that lay at the mouth of a turbulent river, a cry rang out, "BOY OVERBOARD!" A crowd gathered and anxious eyes looked out over the rushing water to see the figure of the drowning boy. Every anxious mother cried, "Is it my boy?"

A rope was brought, and the strongest swimmer in the village volunteered to rescue the drowning lad. Tying one end around his waist, he threw the other end into the crowd and plunged into the raging waters. Eagerly everyone watched him breast the tide with strong, sure strokes, and a cheer went up when he reached the boy and grasped him safely in his powerful grip. "Pull in the rope! Pull in the rope!" he shouted over the furious waters.

The villagers looked from one to another. "Who is holding the rope?" they asked. No one was holding the rope. In the excitement of watching the rescue, the end of the rope had slipped into the water and disappeared. Powerless to help, they watched not just one but two precious lives go down because no one had made it their business to hold the end of the rope!

Millions perish for eternity because there is no one to hold the rope!

*　　*　　*

Having heard and responded to God's call to world-wide missions, I can't even begin to tell you how vitally important intercession is for me as a missionary. As sure as day follows night, I can expect someone to greet me after a mission with, "Joy, I don't know what was going on, but the Lord woke me up to pray for you!" And then the Holy Spirit would remind me of one harrowing episode or another that would coincide with the timing of this person's prayers. People holding the rope cause miraculous things to happen because God answers prayer. As William Carey is so often quoted as saying, "Expect great things from God; attempt great things for God." Prayer is our greatest work.

It was with the assurance that we would have Rope Holders in place that my husband, Wes, and I accepted a call to stand alongside the pastors of the churches in Estonia in 1993. Having sensed the Lord was about to change the season we were in, our hearts were prepared to respond. Having pastored our two Methodist congregations over the previous seven years, we had at least some experience in shepherding a flock. However, nothing and no one other than the Holy Spirit could have prepared us for what we would encounter in the newly-liberated country of Estonia, so recently freed from the oppression of the Soviet government.

Located on the east coast of the Baltic Sea in northern Europe, the mainland Republic of Estonia is bordered on the north by the Gulf of Finland, to the south by Latvia, and to the east by Russia, with an additional 2,222 small islands afloat in the Baltic Sea. With a population of about 1.5 million at that time, most of the people had no faith tradition or religious affiliation; a good many of them had never heard about Jesus.

With a complicated history of being governed by Scandinavian and Teutonic rulers, Estonia had finally declared their independence after World War II, having fought a war against Bolshevik Russia as well as Baltic German forces. With the Tartu Peace Treaty of 1920, Estonia enjoyed a brief twenty years of autonomy until they were occupied by the Soviet Union in 1940, followed by Nazi Germany in 1941. The Soviets reoccupied the nation in 1944 and retained dictatorship until the Soviet Union was dissolved in 1991.

Ravaged by World War II, Estonian seaports, cities, railways, and industry were either completely destroyed or seriously devastated. People who were able to flee to Western Europe abandoned homes and businesses in favor of freedom. Those who did not demonstrate loyalty to the Soviet communist government were arrested and executed. Over 20,000 dissidents were deported to Siberia.

In 1946, shortly after the end of World War II, British Prime Minister Winston Churchill delivered a speech declaring that an "iron curtain" was descending over Europe, although he was not the first to have employed that term. Still, the phrase came into common usage as it represented the ideological, economic, and political sepa- ration between Eastern and Western Europe and seemed to coincide with the onset of the Cold War. Churchill's term described the invisible yet nearly tangible barrier separating communist from capitalist countries through radical Soviet control and oppression.

While the Iron Curtain was not an actual physical barrier, it was certainly bolstered by the Berlin Wall beginning in 1961. A fortified concrete structure built right down the middle of Germany's capital city of Berlin, the wall reinforced who would live in freedom and who would live under oppression. Fortified with barbed wire, spikes, land mines, and armed guards, the 96-mile-long, nearly 12-foot-high wall was a constant symbol of subjugation to those who had already lost so much.

Known post-war as the Estonia Soviet Socialist Republic, this beleaguered country followed the dictates of the Communist party under Joseph Stalin until his death in 1953. The Estonians grew more and more concerned over the extent to which Russian domination was infiltrating their cultural identity and even their language. By 1981, the Russian language was being taught, beginning in the preschools. Alcoholism became a significant public health issue. The national identity was so compromised that the Estonians feared their culture would not survive.

During the 1980's, Mikhail Gorbachev, president of the U.S.S.R. (Union of Soviet Socialist Republics), became the mastermind behind the restructuring of Russia known as perestroika. He began to institute fundamental changes in the economic and political structures of Russia. But the suddenness of these reforms, coupled with growing instability both within and outside the Soviet Union, helped contribute to the eventual collapse of the U.S.S.R. in 1991.

Unknown to the Estonians during this era of change taking place in the 1980's, the finger of God was miraculously at work on their behalf. Because they still had little contact with the outside world, the Estonian citizens could not have known that the president of the United States, Ronald Reagan, stood in front of the Brandenburg Gate near the Berlin Wall on June 12, 1987, passionately admonishing Mikhail Gorbachev with these words: "Mr. Gorbachev, tear down this wall!" And on November 9, 1989, that wall was ordered to come down. Still, it would take years for the physical wall to be dismantled and even more time for the people to come to terms with what it meant to be free.

In an attempt to retain their identity and regain their autonomy, new political parties in Estonia were being formed almost daily. As the people banded together, their solidarity resulted in the establishment of a Congress in 1990. All of their efforts were rewarded in a referendum in March, 1991, when the citizens of Estonia voted to become an independent nation. Confirmed on August 20, 1991, the Estonians were finally released from Russian domination. Yet it would not be until August 31, 1994 that the Soviet armed troops would finally withdraw from the country, leaving them truly free to pursue political and economic ties with Western Europe and the rest of the world.

~

It is for freedom that Christ has set us free. Stand firm, then, and do not let yourselves be burdened again by a yoke of slavery.   GALATIANS 5:1, NIV

MISSION: ESTONIA
PART TWO

"Behold, I send an Angel before you to keep you
in the way and to bring you into the place which
I have prepared."   EXODUS 23:20, NKJV

WITH THE COLLAPSE and dissolution of the Soviet Union
on December 31, 1991, an opportunity opened for the
evangelical church to further the gospel in countries that
had been deprived of any teaching about Jesus for anywhere between five and seven decades. World Methodist
Evangelism, a unit of the World Methodist Council,
had supported the Methodist Church of Estonia during
Communist occupation and now wanted to stand even
more strongly with the Christian leaders in Estonia who
had so courageously persevered and even thrived during
that oppressive regime. We were given the opportunity to
go and serve as missionaries alongside pastors and leaders
in this newly-freed nation.

Thankful to not be a material girl, I still had to consider
the many needs of our little family of four as we made plans
to cross the Atlantic and settle into a whole new world of
unknowns. Storing most of our earthly possessions in my
parents' barn in rural Georgia, we loaded 23 U-Haul card-
board boxes with essential clothes, books, pots and pans,

bed and bath linens, and a few of the kids' favorite toys. Knowing there would probably not be anything like our Dollar Tree stores in Estonia, I added some inexpensive little games and toys for their birthdays and Christmas, along with a few Duncan Hines cake mixes so at least something would taste familiar in our holiday celebrations.

With our daughter Hannah being three years old and son Caleb just one, our hearts were torn at the prospect of pulling these little ones away from their adoring grandparents. But even at their young ages, they seemed to understand we were all about our Father's business and were in this adventure together. Waving goodbye to our beloved family in Atlanta with more than token tears, we boarded our transatlantic flight to Amsterdam.

Blessedly, both of our children were born with a sense of adventure and adapted well to unfamiliar circumstances, including air travel. Armed with books, games, blankies, and whatever else would fit into our backpacks, we let them snuggle in our laps or visit other passengers in the aisles. Nursing Caleb helped to alleviate the discomfort of air pressure changes during takeoff and landing. Most of all, we focused on having fun together as a family.

After a brief layover in Helsinki, Finland, we were relieved to think our long journey would soon be over. Boarding a little puddle-jumper for our final flight across the Gulf of Finland to our destination city of Tallinn, Wes and I were a little unnerved to see these words written on the metal of the old Russian Aeroflot plane inside a 15x15 inch red square: CUT HERE IN CASE OF EMERGENCY. Not very reassuring for travel-weary parents of toddlers.

Greeted at the airport by those faithful saints who had pressed on through years of Communist oppression, we were warmly embraced and welcomed to their world. I had to almost pinch myself when I realized we were like pioneers, among the first Westerners to enter this new frontier after the Iron Curtain had been lifted. What a privilege to be able to freely proclaim the name of Jesus!

Stepping out of the airport into the frigid March air, it was kind of shocking to realize the average daily temperature in Tallinn at that time of year was literally half that of Atlanta. Leaving a balmy 68 degrees the day before for a high of 34 plus snow-lined streets at least temporarily revived our travel-weary bodies.

Taken by our hosts to the house provided for us, we were thankful to find a first-floor garage next to a small living room and office. Upstairs were three bedrooms and a kitchen. We soon learned that we were especially blessed to have a flushing toilet, a luxury in Estonia at the time. The story was that the contractor who built the house wanted to woo back his wife, who had left Estonia for refuge in Finland. Thinking indoor plumbing just might do the trick, he was disappointed to find his bribe was insufficient, and ended up following her to Finland. However, he rented the apartment to us and we were forever grateful.

As we gradually acclimated to life in Tallinn, we observed that about half the people spoke Estonian, and half spoke Russian. Through whatever means we could, including sign language, we began to communicate with our new friends. Thankfully, the superintendent of the Methodist church in Tallinn when we arrived, Olav

Parnamets and his wife, Urve, spoke English, Estonian, and Russian. They had led Estonian-speaking believers for many years in the midst of Soviet occupation, and were frequently taken to KGB headquarters for interrogation and even imprisoned for their faith.

It was quite an education for me to hear their stories of persecution, having grown up in a free country where we could speak our minds and worship God without fear of censorship, imprisonment, torture, or even loss of life. I asked my new friends how such a relatively small group of Communist leaders could gain such control over the masses. The answer was through intimidation: holding people captive at gunpoint in front of family members, threatening to rape or kill them or harm their children if they didn't comply.

One of the Communist strategies when they first came to power was to force the Russians to go into the other Soviet-led countries and work as marginalized servants for the purpose of mixing up the cultures and languages so everyone would theoretically become similar. People were forced to work side by side under harsh conditions in factories, but prohibited from any conversation with those around them. For some, it was even worse. Many citizens of Estonia, Latvia, and Lithuania were shoved onto cattle cars and shipped to Siberia, where some of them were killed. It was all about control.

Wes and I started to realize what a privilege we had in coming to Estonia so soon after its liberation. Even though the people were now technically free, the mentality of Soviet occupation remained. In certain parts of the world where elephants are raised, the training process involves "crushing," which puts the young calves in a cage, tied with ropes to restrict movement. They gradually become less and less aware of their strength because it can't be put to the test. This is what Communism does to humans. It tries to crush them.

When we first arrived, many of the people we met were still afraid to even sign their names to any type of document, fearing for their lives. We lived near the port city of Paldiski, site of a Soviet nuclear submarine base, and civilians were not permitted near there, nor were they informed of what was happening on that base. With everything being kept top secret by the Russians, all the average citizen in Estonia knew was that there was the potential for nuclear radioactivity as the base was being dismantled after independence was decreed. A lack of information only served to fuel the level of their fear. But there is always a remnant of overcomers, and we had the unique opportunity to meet and partner with them in bringing the gospel to Estonia.

The Russian-speaking contingent of Methodists in Estonia was led by Georg and Katya Lanberg, but it was more challenging to communicate with them because Georg spoke Russian and Estonian, and Katya's primary language was Russian. No English on their part meant I needed to become proficient in Estonian fast. But their hearts spoke the universal language of love. Just thinking of Georg and Katya brings to mind the Hebrews 11 "Hall of Faith," especially verse 28: *the world was not worthy of them.*

So many faithful ones are not recognized in this life, but God has planned something better for them.

Trying to find our way around this strange but wonderful new place was especially challenging because there were absolutely no signs, so you had no idea what kind of building was in front of you. During the Soviet occupation, the Communists had labeled all the buildings in Russian, but the newly-liberated Estonians didn't want any reminders of their former rulers, so they tore them all down.

One Sunday after church service (we'd only been in Estonia a few weeks), I asked an elderly woman in her 80's what was in the building across the street from us. She said she didn't know, and I looked at her incredulously. She had lived there all her life! But then she explained, "You are an American, so you ask questions. But we were never allowed to do that. We might have been at one place and told that something existed in another place, but we were never permitted to ask how to get there. The Soviets told us where we would live, what bus we would get on, what market we could buy food at, where we would work, and how we would get there." This was mind-boggling for us as we tried to understand and fit into the culture, knowing the heartache of all they had endured.

So, all I could do was learn my way around by knocking on doors. Not being a timid person, I just went door to door, not knowing who or what might be behind them. Sometimes it would be someone selling heads of cabbage; sometimes it was a private apartment and they were in the process of changing clothes. *Excuse me* was a good phrase for me to learn in Estonian.

Since there were no supermarkets at the time, I had to go to a different kind of market for everything we needed.

I might have to take a bus somewhere to find potatoes, another to buy flour, and still another to find sugar. Thankfully, we were able to purchase a used vehicle, despite the fact that only 20% of the Estonians owned cars.

Another memorable Sunday after church, our family was invited to a birthday party for one of the children in the congregation. Although the Communists had removed many customs from normal daily life, one of the things they didn't prohibit was birthday parties. Not wanting to go empty-handed, I grabbed a little watercolor set and coloring book I had bought at the Dollar Store before we left the States, something I had originally intended to give our daughter but sensed I needed to bring to the birthday girl. What completely undid me was how our hosts perceived this gift as extravagant, the most special present their child had received. So humbling.

The typical fare for an Estonian gathering usually featured open-faced sandwiches made with small rounds of a hard, dark bread spread with butter, then topped with sliced cucumber and raw fish. This was always a treat for them, but not on my top ten list of palate pleasers. Or even top twenty. Still, I politely nibbled at the edge of the bread until a moment when no one was looking, when I jammed the little sandwich into my coat pocket so I wouldn't offend our hosts by leaving it uneaten.

Wes and I had agreed that he would take the children home while I went shopping for groceries after the party, so I got on the tram to the market I knew would have what we needed. I watched with curiosity as a big, burly Russian man with two humongous dogs, each certainly weighing more than I did, got on the tram car that was already packed like sardines. With probably 100 people crammed in, not to mention assorted boxes, bags, and other containers, the man and his beasts edged in close to me. Restrained by leashes that looked like the tractor chains my daddy used on our farm, I figured these dogs were used to getting their way.

Suddenly, the beasts started nosing their way up and down my coat, growling with a deep, low rumble as they sniffed the fishy contents of my pocket. Knowing that sandwich would be just an appetizer en route to my hip-bone, I pushed my way through the crowd and jumped off the tram at the next stop, having no idea where on earth I was.

It took me quite a while to get my bearings and figure out how to get back to our apartment, but I did learn a life lesson that day for those of us in missions. Never, ever leave home without a tissue, napkin, or plastic bag. This is basic survival for the mission field. People are always watching to see if you are willing to eat what they eat. Most of the time, I do—or at least I try. But sometimes I've had to ask Jesus to help me not throw up, and He does. I've sampled cow's blood, maggots and worms, goat guts, jungle rats, you name it. But if you just can't stomach it, toss it in the bag.

As I began to learn the Estonian language, with a smattering of Russian on the side, it was such fun to watch our kids pick it up so easily. With both Estonian and Russian neighbors around us, the exposure was constant. Outgoing little Hannah would greet everyone with a cheerful *Tere!,* which means hello, and then turn to her Russian friends with a similar welcome, *Privyet!* Everyone seemed to appreciate her efforts as she assumed her part in our family's calling. But Caleb was quietly taking it all in, eager to imitate his sister.

So glad that a group of friends from a supporting church in the northern U.S. had the foresight to send us hand-me-down jackets, hats, gloves, and boots for the kids, I'd bundled them up one frigid day to go out and play in the snow. With a vast forest behind us, full of beautiful birch and fir trees laced with snowy white like you'd see in the Pacific Northwest states, the children had lots of space to run around and play with the neighbors.

Just learning to talk, Caleb was listening simultaneously to one group of Estonian children and another pack of Russian kids. Suddenly, he spouted out a full sentence with words in English, Estonian, and Russian. Although none of his playmates could understand what he was saying, he was pleased as punch, so proud of himself.

Of course, our kids helped the neighbor children learn English, too. When our neighbors' cat had several kittens, they gifted us with a black one and a white one. Letting our children decide their names, we were amused that they chose Blackie and Whitey. But these kittens soon became famous because all the neighbor kids could say their names and were thrilled that they were speaking English. A win-win, for sure.

It was great to enjoy such lighthearted times, especially because we really missed our family and friends back in the States. Whenever we got mail from parents, friends, or prayer partners, it was such a boost to our day, especially if they tucked in a few sticks of gum or a couple of balloons for the kids. A dear older couple who were members of one of our partner churches were so faithful to write often. Gearing their letters to things that would appeal to our kids, they'd send serial stories about their dog, Smoky. *Smoky was chasing squirrels today in our backyard and almost got one, but the mama squirrel scratched his face.* The kids would look forward to the next episode of the adventures of Smoky. So cute.

As missionaries in a country where luxuries were in short supply, we hooted and hollered when we received packages containing boxes of Cheerios, cans of tuna, bags of candy—those familiar things you don't think twice about throwing into your grocery cart. Things like coloring books and crayons for the kids, little games and small toys all meant so much because they came from home and hearts that cared for us. Since we did have a small portable TV set and VCR machine with an adaptor, it was awesome when churches and individuals sent us tapes of *Barney, Sesame Street, Bibleman, Do-Nut Man,* and *Focus on the Family* shows for the kids and us.

Seemingly little things were actually a big deal, helping us to remain content and feel cared for as we were so far away from home. A woman in one of our supporting churches had given me a recipe for making missionary-friendly flapjacks, or pancakes, using maple flavoring I could mix with water and sugar to make a tasty substitute for maple syrup. We'd also been given tips on how to use simple, readily-available ingredients like vinegar and baking soda as inexpensive, effective cleaning supplies. We learned to make do with whatever we had and be grateful for what came our way through the goodness of God and the gifts of others.

What a gift of encouragement every note or letter was to us! Knowing we were being thought of and prayed for was invaluable. Every little excursion to the post office was exciting for our family, knowing there might be something waiting for us from those at home. I wish I could personally acknowledge every individual who has encouraged and prayed for us through the years, but please know your contributions have made all the difference.

When people would sometimes write or say to me, "I can't believe the sacrifice you're making," I'd be grateful for the compliment but my response would be, "I'm just an extension of other people." I'm a member of the body of Christ, just as you are. All of us depend on one another, however and wherever we are serving. But Scripture says people have beautiful feet if they are helping to send someone else through prayer and/or practical support. All the miracles and the evidence of God's hand on things is due to the power of fervent intercession. We can do nothing without prayer.

⌯

The Lord is near to all who call upon Him, to all who call upon Him in truth. He will fulfill the desire of those who fear Him; He also will hear their cry and save them. PSALM 145:18-19, NKJV

MISSION: ESTONIA
PART THREE

The Lord is a refuge for the oppressed, a stronghold in times of trouble. Those who know your name will trust in you, for you, Lord, have never forsaken those who seek you.   PSALM 9:9-10, NIV

Worshiping with our new friends and colleagues, Olav and Urve Parnamets and Georg and Katya Lanberg, was always such a blessing! Because of the Estonian/Russian bi-cultural background, all worship services were held in both languages. The Tallinn Methodist Church was actually comprised of two congregations within one local church. Services were held back-to-back in the Estonian and Russian languages on Sunday mornings, and then again in the evenings.

The Methodists were blessed to be able to rent a Seventh-day Adventist church building for gatherings, so convenient because the Adventists always hold services on Saturday. We also had multiple requests to visit other churches scattered in rural areas of Estonia. The people were always so honored and even thrilled that we would leave the capital city to come and share Jesus with them. But we knew that's exactly what Jesus would do, and we wanted to see the country as well as visit different congregations.

How exciting it was to see the dynamic faith of these parishioners after so many years of repression! Wes and I were greatly influenced by the lives and works of the Wesley brothers, John and Charles, and drew on their vast teachings and hymns as we preached and taught different congregations. As the majority of the churches there were Methodist, some had heard the Wesley name, but others had not.

Starting at the very beginning, we explained that the Methodist movement was so named because it is methodical. The founder, John Wesley, methodically preached salvation, holiness, and a second work of grace—being filled with the Holy Spirit. He emphasized complete surrender to Jesus Christ as well as the importance of spiritual accountability to others. He encouraged the practice of spiritual disciplines such as Bible study, prayer, fasting, and meeting together regularly with likeminded brothers and sisters.

John Wesley encouraged gathering in small groups weekly, as well as meeting as a society with several groups coming together each month for the purpose of loving accountability. "Are you reading the word every day? Are you praying and memorizing Scripture? Is your soul prospering?" These were the kinds of questions the early Methodists would ask each other, the same things we know are important to us as believers today, but sometimes concepts we talk about more than we actually do.

Wesley's faith did not remain inside the walls of a church. He would rise at 5:00 or 5:30 each morning, taking to the streets of London and beyond to preach to factory workers, farmers, and any who would listen to the gospel. He became known for saying, "Do all the good you can, by all the means you can, in all the ways you can, in all the places you can, at all the times you can, to all the people you can, as long as ever you can." I have always been inspired by that and try to live up to it.

John Wesley's younger brother, Charles, who helped him found the Methodist movement, was best known for his approximately 6,500 inspired hymns, including some of our favorites like *Hark! the Herald Angels Sing, O for a Thousand Tongues to Sing, Christ the Lord is Risen Today,* and *And Can It Be?*. Charles also formed the "Holy Club" at Oxford University, which his brother John later joined, along with evangelist George Whitefield.

Looking at the extraordinary lives of these two Wesley brothers, you can't help but wonder what kind of parents they had. Their father, Samuel, was an Anglican clergyman who encouraged his children to pursue God, but it was primarily the influence of their mother, Susanna, that shaped their lives. Having given birth to nineteen children, with ten surviving to adulthood, she made it a priority to spend one-on-one time with each of her children every week, encouraging them to grow in their love of Jesus.

As one who hungrily read and studied God's word, Susanna Wesley became a teacher of the word, even at a time when women were not allowed to do that. It was as if her passion for Jesus could not be contained, and she had to share what was in her heart with everyone in her world. When the milkman made his rounds, he might see and hear Susanna through the window, reading her Bible and crying out to God. Neighbors began to gather in the Wesley kitchen for spiritual food that would sustain them. Her yielded life introduced everyone she met to Jesus Christ.

Known by the Church of England as a non-conforming dissenter, Susanna Wesley died without being recognized by the church she and her husband had served. When the politically-correct Anglican pastors were preaching or holding meetings, they would address matters in people-pleasing ways, but not Susanna. If it was not consistent with the Word of God, she would boldly correct them and assert the truth.

If you ever happen to be in London, England, I encourage you to visit Wesley's Chapel on City Road in northeast London. There is a little townhouse surrounded now by modern office buildings where John Wesley lived the last 12 years of his life. Inside are many of his belongings and a prayer room where heavenly transactions changed the world. Right across the street is a cemetery, Bunhill Fields, where Susanna Wesley is buried. I love the knowledge that she rests not in obscurity, but in the company of other saintly nonconformists and radical dissenters like John Bunyan, Sir Isaac Watts, Daniel Defoe, and William Blake.

As the women of the Tallinn congregation heard about the Wesleys, they were eager to learn more. They approached me, asking if we could have a retreat centering around the life of Susanna Wesley. It was the first of its kind for them, and a great joy for me to lead. As these precious people ventured out in their walk with Jesus, the opportunity for other "firsts" began to come to us, one of which was summer camps for children and youth.

Although a bit complicated because everything had to be doubled to accommodate both the Estonian and Russian languages, we loved working with the outstanding Estonian leaders to help organize this camp. There would be two weeks of children's camp in Estonian, then two weeks in Russian. One week of youth camp in Estonian, one week in Russian. But the way the Lord provided for all the details was truly a miracle.

During the Soviet occupation, the Communists had forced citizens to live in communal housing; in rural areas, they were called communal farms. However, instead of a typical farmhouse building, they built tall, block-like structures where hundreds or even thousands of people lived together. With minimal provision for sanitation, they were like tenements in early twentieth-century America that housed newly-arrived immigrants.

Forced to go out on what had once been their own land but was now owned by the government, these people would work for wages that would then be turned over to the state. Their compensation for hard labor would be a government ration of the crops they had planted and harvested with their own hands. The number of potatoes they received would be determined by the Communists.

In the northeast corner of Estonia bordering Russia, there was a large power plant that provided electricity for the entire northwestern quadrant of Russia. Whenever there was a big government function, the Soviets would gather at a camp located within these power plant communities. Beginning at age six, all the children would be forced to go for two weeks of Communist indoctrination, where they would be taught how to be loyal to Lenin. But when freedom came, that land with the camp buildings was abandoned, becoming a field of weeds.

Yet what the enemy intended for evil, the Lord is able to use for good. Thrilled to get permission to use this camp, the Christian leaders got together and named it Camp Gideon. With limited resources, they worked creatively to use everything available. Thrilled to get permission to use this camp, the Christian leaders got together and named it Camp Gideon. With our resources severely limited, almost non-existent, we had to get super creative with what we had. One woman provided an old bed sheet on which she painted *Camp Gideon* in Russian, and we hoisted it up on a pedestal to serve as the camp flag. It was such a blessing to raise that sheet flag over a land that had been used for so many years for the devil's work, claiming it for Jesus!

Although many were familiar with cultural Christianity, there were some who didn't understand what "Christian" meant. Our leadership team said, "Well, we might get a hundred," but we really had no idea how many to expect. That first day as we sat there eating our lunch of potato soup, children began peering through the windows, their eager expressions conveying anticipation of what was surely to come! In the end, the worship team had far more than 200 children at camp.

As they learned the Jesus songs we taught them, the same songs most of us learned in Sunday school and VBS, and absorbed the stories of Jesus from the Bible, they couldn't wait to go home and share them with their families. Parents and grandparents, who had sent their children to this Christian camp out of curiosity, began hearing about God the Father and about Jesus His Son, who died so the world might be saved. Our camp kids were becoming little evangelists.

After camp, we had other exciting "firsts" for the churches—open baptisms. In Estonia, they prefer to baptize by immersion, but since it is near the North Pole in Santa Claus land, rivers and creeks are frozen solid in the winter. Waiting for summertime, when at least a corner of the lake or part of the river or creek had thawed, all those who had gotten saved the previous year gathered to be baptized.

With all the men going into the bushes and trees on one side, and all the women doing the same on the other side, they would remove their clothes and put on white baptismal robes they had fashioned out of sheets. Entering the still-frigid waters with great intent, each one would emerge with new life as they were baptized in the name of the Father, Son, and Holy Spirit. "*Slava bogu! Glory to God!*" the Russian speakers would exclaim as they rose out of the icy water.

While it is awesome to witness anyone coming into the kingdom of God, what touched me most deeply was to see the precious, precious elderly people in their eighties and nineties yield their lives to Jesus. Having lived under Communist oppression most of their lives, to see them experience the truest kind of liberation was the greatest reward for me. Jesus desires that none would perish, and that all would have everlasting life.

~

It is for freedom that Christ has set us free. Stand firm, then, and do not let yourselves be burdened again by a yoke of slavery. GALATIANS 5:1, NIV

MISSION: ESTONIA
PART FOUR

Jesus answered, "My teaching is not my own.
It comes from the one who sent me."   JOHN 7:16, NIV

ABOUT TWO MONTHS after our arrival in Tallinn, pastors from throughout the country gathered for a prayer meeting to discern God's plans for the future of the church in Estonia. Sensing the depth of the need to hear correctly and prompted by obedience to the Holy Spirit, many were on their knees, petitioning God for specific guidance. Others were lying prostrate before the Lord in adoration and earnest supplication. Half the pastors were praying in Russian, half in Estonian. Whatever the language, everyone was led by the Spirit.

The superintendent of the Methodist church, Olav Parnamets, quietly made his way around the room, asking each pastor, "What is God saying to you?" He was not asking for their opinion on what God might be doing in our midst; he was asking for the specific words God was impressing on their hearts. To a person, the answer was, "Now is the time to start a seminary here."

The last theological seminary in the Baltic states, located to the south of Estonia in the country of Latvia, had been active half a century before but was shut down by the

Communists during World War II. Since that time, no formal training had been available for pastors. However, a firm foundation had been quietly forming as faithful Methodist leaders Alexander Kuum, Hugo Oengo, Georg Lanberg, and Olav Parnamets labored underground to teach and disciple students. As those gathered at this pivotal meeting agreed unanimously that it was time to start a seminary, we knew it would be built on their shoulders, by the grace of God.

One of my favorite stories related to the seminary began about a year earlier on our first trip to Estonia. Taking a field trip by bus from Tallinn to the capital city of Riga, Latvia, with our new Methodist superintendent-friend Olav, we were to attend a meeting with his counterpart there. With our new superintendent-friend Olav, we planned a meeting with his counterpart in Latvia. We were looking forward to seeing where their former seminary had been before the Communists destroyed it during World War II, and share the vision for a new seminary in Estonia.

Despite the proximity of these two Baltic nations that share a border, their languages are radically different. Olav could not speak a word of Latvian, but he could speak some Russian, so we were counting on him to be able to communicate, one way or another. We would spend two nights in Latvia, but we knew it would take many hours to get there.

Road-weary after hours on a bus that could have used a new suspension system, we finally arrived at the border between Estonia and Latvia, only to encounter a line of buses and boxy Russian Lada cars as far as our eyes could see. At long last, some uniformed soldiers boarded our bus with AK-47 assault rifles, not accustomed to seeing

Estonians because they hadn't been allowed to travel during Soviet occupation.

The soldiers asked everyone to surrender their passports so they could check everything in their office. During what became a very long wait, I got restless and decided to get off the bus for a few minutes to see if I could take a picture of the soldiers in uniform, something authentically Latvian to remember this visit. Approaching two of them, I tried to say a few words in Estonian, but they didn't understand anything I said and just laughed. So, I got into the spirit of it and started to try to teach them some English.

Pointing to myself, I said, "I am Joy." And then I pointed to their chests and said, "You. You." But they had absolutely no clue as to what I meant. I kept going back and forth, saying, "Joy" and "You." Finally, I managed to learn their names, Igor and Ginks, and they realized at last what I was trying to teach them.

Still hoping for a photo op, I decided the picture would look a whole lot better if these guys had their guns on display. The trouble was, their AK-47's were slung across their backs. Since I couldn't communicate my plan to them, I just reached around one of them to grab the gun for my photo shoot (sorry for the pun). Suddenly, everyone standing there went nuts, jumping back in terror, as the people on our bus yelled out the windows, "Joy, are you CRAZY?!"

But Igor and Ginks realized I just wanted them to model their guns for the picture, and started laughing uncontrollably as if it were the funniest thing they'd ever seen. However, I got a whole lot of grief from my traveling companions when I got back on the bus.

Finally arriving in Riga for our meetings, we were warmly welcomed by the Latvian superintendent, who was so happy to see us. It was difficult, though, to see how the Communists had appropriated the sanctuary of the Latvian church, turning it into a Soviet boxing ring during the occupation. I can only imagine the desolation a pastor and congregation would feel to lose their church in this way.

After two nights in Riga, it was time to get back on that bus and return to Tallinn. On one of our stops on the way back, I noticed a little scooter, similar to the Razor model that so many kids have these days, but made of very old-fashioned, heavy iron metal. It was the equivalent of only four U.S. dollars, so I quickly bought it for our children. They loved that scooter and both rode it until they outgrew it. It was so sturdy, I hauled it back with us to the States and actually still have it. Maybe we'll have grandkids who will ride it one day.

Arriving at the Latvian/Estonian border that evening, we came upon another seemingly-endless line of vehicles, backed up for what would certainly amount to hours. Cars, buses, freight trucks, all with their windows open, their occupants complaining loudly—it was total chaos. Suddenly, our bus doors flipped open and some soldiers with high-beam flashlights got on. Shining their lights into every corner, speaking in sharp, loud tones of voice. their high beams suddenly focused on me.

Unexpected peals of laughter began emanating from the soldiers as they strode through the bus in my direction. Because it was dark, I couldn't make out their faces, but all at once, their lights revealed it was my two buddies, Igor and Ginks!

"Joy! JOY!" they exclaimed, (their English lesson evidently successful, since they remembered my name!) as they reached over, attempting to hug me. They motioned for my passport and I figured they had the authority to get us all out of there quickly, so I pointed to my stunned travel mates. They collected their passports as well.

Within minutes, Igor and Ginks came back with everything stamped, personally escorting us around all of the vehicles that were backed up for miles. Now the same travel companions who'd thought I was crazy were pretty impressed by this red carpet treatment. I held my tongue from saying, "I told you so," but it really did pay to be kind and friendly to these young men.

When we returned to Estonia a year later, Wes and I earnestly prayed over the myriad details of this endeavor. We knew we would need financial backing, a facility in which to meet, trained faculty members who spoke Estonian and/or Russian, equipment for translation, and lots of textbooks. In this pre-internet era, we would have to locate hard copies of books that we knew would not be found in Estonia. We would, in short, need many miraculous manifestations of the power of God. So that is exactly what we prayed for.

Although we had raised our own missionary support to pay rent and buy food for our family, we knew there would not be any excess to finance a seminary. Seeking the Lord's counsel, we were led to write letters to all the individuals and churches in the States who were sponsoring/

supporting us, and sent them on their way across the ocean, stamped with our fervent prayers. Sharing our vision for the seminary, we suggested they each consider helping to sponsor a student. Having no idea what our expenses might be, we speculated it might cost $1000 a year per student.

Having arrived in Estonia that March, our transformational prayer meeting had taken place on May 5, leaving us just three months to plan for the seminary's projected opening in August. The Methodist Church of Estonia leadership team and Wes asked the Estonian pastors to pray we would have 30 students to begin the seminary, hoping there might possibly be that many who would be interested. But we had underestimated God's recruiting ability and eventually had 52 students enrolled in the first class.

Responses to our letters requesting student sponsorship began to come, with many partners eager to help finance this new endeavor. The leadership team enlisted Estonian church members to find families with homes in our area who might host the prospective students. The idea was for the students to come weekly by bus to Tallinn for classes, stay with a local family, and return to their homes on weekends. Cooks would be provided to prepare food for them in the compact space we would call our headquarters.

Wes agreed to be the Academic Dean of the seminary, as well as to mentor the Estonian pastor who would be the president. I agreed to serve as a member of the faculty, and we both continued to come alongside pastors of our church as encouragers and frequent guest preachers. Having prayed for more faculty members to be provided for us, we were still completely amazed by God's incredible answers. Two young Estonian women who had been sent by OM International to study the Bible in Sweden appeared back on the scene at exactly the right time. One had earned a degree in Old Testament, the other in New Testament. One was very fluent in Estonian, while the other was fluent in Russian. And both spoke fluent English. This was really miraculous provision!

Having amazingly been granted a license to operate a seminary, we received approval from the Methodist Church of Estonia to use one room in their building headquarters, located in the Old Town section of Tallinn. But we still needed teaching resources. With our fellow pastors scouring the country for any Christian materials in the Estonian language, they were coming up dry—such evidence of the Communist's eradication of anything and everything testifying to Jesus.

There was an old Lutheran church in the southern part of Estonia that was boarded up, with guards posted on site to keep people from looking through the windows. If anyone dared sneak a peek, their names were taken and they were punished. Ironically, it spoke to me of the Communists' awareness of the power of Jesus Christ and the gospel. If the people were to see a cross, a Bible, or maybe even a candlestick, they might be curious as to what these things represented. This would create a problem.

But in that little church, a single copy of *The Confessions of Saint Augustine,* translated into Estonian, was found by some church members. We were also blessed to have access to the notes and books of the founding faculty. Wes and

I both had our class notes from Asbury Seminary, which we'd had translated into Estonian and Russian, but were meeting with lots of obstacles, particularly struggling to find any Christian books written in Russian.

Once again, the Lord prospered our prayers, moving the hearts of those in the Wesleyan world we didn't even realize were watching. Since we had no reliable outside communication, we gradually began to realize the whole world had been praying for the Soviet Union to crumble, a very pregnant moment for the church world as they waited to see what God would do. Eager to be part of the rebirth of the church behind the Iron Curtain, the body of Christ responded.

Help began pouring in, with one church in the States providing money for books, and another offering some used translation equipment. This enabled us to hold classes in English with simultaneous translation in either Estonian or Russian. Everyone would have a headset in addition to a hand-held device, so if we were teaching in English and someone asked a question in Russian, everyone would have to change the handset channel in order to understand. While it was a bit primitive, the Lord blessed it and made everything work.

Another potential obstacle we had anticipated concerned the inherent animosity between the Estonians and Russians because of decades of occupation and oppression. How would we manage both groups in the same classroom if they couldn't get along? Once again, the Holy Spirit was mightily at work as our Counselor. When questions were asked by the students, they began to appreciate what they had in common with the other faction, rather than focus on their differences. Someone might say, "Wow, I never knew you were my brother/sister in the Lord, because my parents taught me to hate you. But you know the same Jesus I know!" The unity of the Spirit began to forge the bond of peace among us.

~

As a prisoner of the Lord, then, I urge you to live a life worthy of the calling you have received. Be completely humble and gentle; be patient, bearing with one another in love. Make every effort to keep the unity of the Spirit through the bond of peace. There is one body and one Spirit— just as you were called to one hope when you were called—one Lord, one faith, one baptism; one God and Father of all, who is over all and through all and in all.

EPHESIANS 4:1-5, NIV

MISSION: ESTONIA
PART FIVE

Whether you turn to the right or to the left, your ears
will hear a voice behind you, saying, "This is the way;
walk in it."
ISAIAH 30:21, NIV

WITH SUMMER BEGINNING TO WANE and the first day
of seminary classes edging a bit too close for comfort, Wes
and I were desperately trying to find Christian books in
Russian for our students. Having heard of a group of people
in Moscow representing several international evangelical
Christian organizations, we learned that they had packages
of five classic Christian books translated into Russian. As
visionaries who had been praying for decades for God to
tear down the Iron Curtain, these people had the foresight
to translate five books from English into Russian, with an
intent to form a little resource library for any Protestant,
Russian-speaking pastor when liberation finally came.

As any type of communication was challenging in
those post-Communist years, given the poor infrastructure, we used a walkie-talkie type of phone to make contact
with outsiders. Finally able to connect with the head of this
group, whom I'll call Ivan, we learned that if we could come
to Moscow, they would give us the books at very minimal
cost, the equivalent of about half a dollar each. Then we

would be able to supply each of our Russian-speaking students with five books for the next three years.

With Moscow being an 18-hour train ride from Tallinn, this really qualified as a major journey that would require someone who could communicate in Russian. Our dear friend, Georg Lanberg, spoke both Estonian and also Russian, so he volunteered to do this for us. However, none of us understood how challenging it would be to find the office in Moscow because the borders of the countries had been closed until so recently and communication was virtually nil. After 18 hours on the train there and back, Georg arrived home, not with the books, but with disappointment written all over his face. Since there were no reliable street signs he could read or even house numbers, he had been unable to find the place and returned empty-handed.

Now with only a measly week or so before the start of classes, we decided Wes would stay in Tallinn with our children, open the school, and teach the class I was scheduled to teach. I would go to Moscow with Georg to pick up the books, hoping the two of us together might be able to locate that office. Wes and I had been trying to learn both Estonian and Russian, so I could communicate with Georg at least a little.

The night before we were to leave, Wes was able to get a very cursory connection with Ivan in Moscow, telling him I would be coming with Georg to pick up the books, asking him to promise two things: that someone who spoke English would meet me/us at the train, and that Ivan would personally see I was escorted back onto the train to Tallinn. With static on the line and our connection quite sporadic, we're still not sure how much of that conversation Ivan was able to understand. But Wes did hear him say, "She probably won't be able to find us because we are illegal and no one knows we're here. Nothing is marked." To which my husband replied, "You just don't know my wife!"

Our plan was to leave the next day on the 11 p.m. train for Moscow, but that same morning, a church member died and Georg was asked to stay in Tallinn to bury him. Still wanting to honor his part in our plan, he offered to send his wife, Katya, in his stead. Now, as much as I loved Georg and Katya, who were like Russian parents to me, Katya didn't speak a word of English or even Estonian. We had absolutely no common language, other than our hands and the love of Jesus. As we rode on the train towards Moscow, she greatly overestimated my beginner's knowledge of Russian, talking up a blue streak. I really didn't have a clue as to what she was saying.

Arriving at the cavernous station in Moscow late in the afternoon, our worn out, addled brains tried to process everything going on around us. What I remember is how monochromatic everything seemed, just shades of gray. Gunmetal gray, tattletale gray. For as far as you could see in any direction, all the buildings looked like big gray blocks. Even the sky was gray. And the clothing the people wore looked as if it were standard government issue, with no one wanting to stand out.

As Katya found a bench nearby and sat down, I scouted the area for our contact, Ivan. No one appeared to be looking for us, so I tried to communicate with Katya that we needed to try to find this man. No matter what gestures or words I used, she kept saying, "*Nyet. Nyet.*" No. She evidently knew something I didn't, so I finally figured I might as well plop down next to her on the bench and just wait.

After sitting there for three hours, Katya suddenly got up and motioned for me to follow her to the subway. Riding underground for an hour, I had no idea where we might end up, but was praying Jesus would take us right to those books. Emerging from the subway at ground level in the dark, all we could see was a much darker version of the shades of gray we had seen earlier in the day.

Walking a few yards, Katya led us to a bus stop, where we boarded a bus and sat for another 45 minutes. Finally pulling my arm to say it was time to get off, I followed Katya as we stepped onto the ground, surrounded by what might just as well have been the last two places we had been. Everything was exactly the same. Gray buildings everywhere the eye could see. I felt kind of like a mouse in a maze.

But this time, Katya spotted an older woman she obviously knew, whom I will call Magda, and they hugged each other. My heart surged with hope, thinking this woman must have the books! They conversed in rapid Russian as we began to make our way through the maze of concrete block buildings, coming to what was evidently her flat. Entering a dark, dingy, narrow elevator, this kind woman took Katya and me up to her apartment, where she served us some very welcome tea. Still unsure of who she really was, I didn't find out until after we returned to Tallinn that Magda was Georg and Katya's only known contact in Russia.

As the two of them continued talking and laughing together, I unobtrusively glanced around the tiny apartment, concluding that I'd be sleeping on the floor that night. Consulting my watch, I was fighting a rising sense of panic, realizing there was no place for the books in this itty-bitty apartment and we had only a limited amount of time to find them. "*Jesus, I need somebody somewhere to pray!*" I silently beseeched Him.

About two hours later, we heard someone knocking on the door. Magda opened it to greet a younger woman about my age, who was inviting her to a prayer meeting that night. Introducing us to this young woman I'll call Olya, our host told her I was from America.

Turning to me, Olya said in perfect English, "Oh, are you from the United States?" Overcome with delight, I said, "Oh, are you an angel from the Lord?" Quickly learning that Olya worked as a translator to facilitate Russian adoptions by English-speaking parents, I sensed she was an answer to my prayers.

"Would you please, please, please help me?!" I asked.

"Yes, of course I will," she said. "But first, would you be willing to come and share with our prayer group this evening what it is like to be a Christian woman in America?"

Naturally, I was thrilled to do this and greatly blessed to spend time with them, and so grateful for my new, English-speaking friend.

After the prayer meeting, Olya was quite willing to make a phone call to Ivan, the man Wes had contacted before Katya and I left for Moscow. Hopefully she would be able to help us get clear directions to find these books.

Then she put Katya on the phone with Ivan so she would hear firsthand how to get there. Finally, he asked to speak to me, since he was also fluent in English.

"I've given Katya the street names. Then you will go down an alley and just count. There are no signs, but count nine buildings, go to an alley, count 5 doors, and we will be the one on the left. When you get there (or maybe he said *if*), knock on the door.

"But this part is very important to remember. When you get to the place on the subway where you're going to come up out of the ground—and remember, this is critical—there will be three exits, with three large sets of stairs. One to the middle, one to the left, and one to the right. You MUST go up the steps to the right. If you do not, you will end up in the wrong place in the city and you will never find us. The way you'll know if you've taken the right staircase is when you come up to street level, you will be able to look up and see the white top of the Moscow Circus tent."

Because he sounded so urgently insistent on the accuracy of these directions, I said, "Could I put Katya back on the phone so you can explain this to her in Russian?"

He answered, "I already did, but I will do it again."

By this time, it was already 2 a.m. and we had yet to lay our heads down for the night. Sleeping fitfully on the floor, I was still so pumped with adrenaline that I was more than ready to hit the ground running first thing in the morning.

Following Ivan's instructions to the letter, Katya and I got on the subway and then off at the appointed stop with the three big stairwells. However, I distinctly remembered Ivan saying, "You must go up the steps to the right." But things got complicated when Katya started going to the left. I kept trying to say to her, "*Nyet*, Katya! We're supposed to go to the right!" But she was just as convinced we were to go to the left.

Wanting with all my heart to honor my friend and show her love and respect, I was so torn. Still, I knew I had heard Ivan correctly, so I doggedly persisted, pulling her up the stairs with me to ground level. Looking all around, I finally saw in the distance a white sort of dome in the sea of gray. The Moscow Circus! Praise Jesus, Katya was not offended in the least. In fact, she started cheering, "*Da, da, da!*" YES!

As Katya peered at the street signs, written of course in the Cyrillic script, she began leading us down the street. Attentively counting buildings, alleys, and doors according to Ivan's precise directions, we came to what we fervently hoped was the right door. Tapping on it like a Morse-code prayer, the door opened to reveal several Russian-speaking people inside a dark room. Still not certain we were in the right place, I simply spoke the name of our contact, Ivan.

"*Da,*" was the only response as we were motioned through two rooms into the cramped space toward the rear of the office. Equipped with money to purchase the books, I realized I would need a private moment to retrieve it, since I'd stashed it in my underwear. We had been warned of thieves who would prey on train passengers, spraying noxious gas under the sleeping berths to lull people to sleep and then rob them.

Meeting Ivan in that back room, he said he would go and get the books, but first asked, "Do you have bribe money?" Appropriately shocked by this blatant request, I must have looked dumbfounded at his question, thinking he was asking for a bribe. But he explained, "Bribery is a way of life here. You're going to need some money to get these books on the train." So relieved that he was not a crook, I listened closely as Ivan went on to say, "If you can get these books across the border, it will be the most we've ever been able to get out of Russia. What happens is when people get to the border of another country, sometimes the customs agents just throw the books off the train— and on occasion, the people with them—because they don't want any reminders of the Soviet regime in their country. Anything Russian is like a curse to them."

With that unexpected but necessary detail, Ivan asked a few of the office staff to join us in prayer. Grasping hands with our brothers and sisters in Jesus, we were fortified by their faith and the knowledge that we had all agreed in prayer and could expect God to see this mission through to completion. One of the team members then offered to transport the books, Katya, and me through Moscow to the train station.

Moving at a crawl through a swarm of Ladas, trucks, buses, and various other obstacles, I was chomping at the bit as I saw the smokestack of a train in the distance. Realistically, there was no earthly way we could make our 4 p.m. departure at this pace. But JESUS could get us there! I uttered a quick petition, *Jesus, we need someone to pray for us right now!*

The One who parted the Red Sea parted the Red Square (well, figuratively speaking), and we arrived just in the nick of time. But we still had 750 books in the van, wrapped in plain, brown-paper bundles, fortunately with no labels identifying what they were. Knowing there was no way Katya, who was much older than I, could lift them, I knew it would be up to me to figure out a plan. Even if I did it by myself, there wasn't enough time to carry them all up the stairs to the waiting train.

Seeing two men leaning against a large cart, leisurely smoking cigarettes, I motioned for them to come over and help me. Laughing in a patronizing sort of way, they could see my distress and knew I wouldn't be able to move those books without their help.

"How many rubles will it cost me for you to take these books to the train?" I asked. They quoted a pretty hefty sum, but I really had no choice and agreed to it, handing them the money. They loaded all the books on their cart, went around a ramp, and met us at the top of the stairs. When I started to unstrap the books from the cart, they pushed me back, saying, "*Nyet! Nyet!*" Rubbing their grimy thumbs with their first two fingers in the universal symbol of greed, I had to shell out several thousand more rubles.

Unfortunately, they didn't keep their end of the bargain, so I was left alone to unload all the books onto the cement platform and lug them to the train. With a woman porter in attendance, I started to lift the first bundle onto the train steps. But instead of helping me, she shoved me back, saying, "*Nyet! Nyet!*" just as the men had done. Ivan's words were proven, not just once but twice, as I doled out another handful of rubles in order to get onto the train with those books.

Sweating profusely, but so grateful to be on that train with our treasures, Katya and I threw ourselves onto the seat in our little berth. With nearly the entire space occupied by the bundles of books, we had no space to lie down, so resigned ourselves to 18 hours upright. But the time was well spent in prayer, knowing we needed to prepare ourselves for what we might encounter at the border.

At around 1:00 a.m., the train crossed the Narva River at the border of Russia and Estonia, stopping for customs officials to come on. Since they were communicating in Russian, I couldn't understand what they were saying. Katya understood, but couldn't communicate it to me. People all around us were screaming, some of them in a drunken stupor, slamming doors, arguing angrily.

Suddenly, the door to our berth opened and a man peered in, seeing nothing but the two of us and all those hundreds of books wrapped in plain brown paper. Having already decided we would tell the truth about what they were, we had also passionately prayed they would not throw the books or us off the train. So, when he asked what they were, all we said was, "Books."

Leaving the berth without a word, he slammed the door shut. Feeling intimidated and fearing he might return, we kept praying for Jesus to help us get through, even as the arguing and slamming of doors persisted outside our door. After about an hour, we heard a sound one wouldn't normally associate with anything positive—the squeal of brakes. But as the train jerked a bit and then began to sway, picking up speed, we were filled with elation. Jesus had heard and helped us!

Pulling into the Tallinn station at daybreak the next morning, Katya and I were met by our families as well as many faithful believers who had waited for decades to have books in their language. We were able to present them with books on Old Testament as well as New Testament history, a Greek textbook, a treatise on hermeneutics (biblical interpretation), and Josh McDowell's classic, *More than a Carpenter*. Seeing these grown men and women weep as we handed them these books in their native language was all the reward we needed.

It was truly a miracle, but God had started Himself a seminary. Today, that little startup is thriving as the largest Methodist theological seminary in Europe by enrollment. Not a tribute to us, but to God's faithfulness to use obedience in the smallest things to bring about His purpose on earth as it is in heaven.

Now to Him who is able to do exceedingly abundantly above all that we ask or think, according to the power that works in us, to Him be glory in the church by Christ Jesus to all generations, forever and ever. Amen.
EPHESIANS 3:20-21, NKJV

MISSION: ESTONIA
PART SIX

Train up a child in the way he should go, and when he is old he will not depart from it.   PROVERBS 22:6, NKJV

I LOVE TO SPEAK ABOUT SUSANNA WESLEY because she had such an incredible gift for effectively combining marriage, motherhood, and ministry. Talk about a Proverbs 31 woman! Her life has inspired me to stretch myself beyond the boundaries of the conventional, daring to venture into what is only possible with God.

Our children, the greatest treasures entrusted to us by God, were not just along for the ride as we traveled the world to spread the gospel. Hannah and Caleb were, and are, integral parts of what we have been called to do. Strong in the Lord, they are both using their creative gifts to glorify Him—Hannah as an artist, and Caleb as a media specialist. We could not be more proud of who they have become as followers of Jesus.

Naturally, missionary parents have some reservations about how life on the field might affect their offspring, but we did our best to help our children adapt to the culture we were serving as well as preserve our own family and cultural traditions. As I mentioned earlier, reading books like Ruth Seamands' *Missionary Mama* opened my understanding to merging cultures and discovering creative ways to make life on the mission field adventurous and fun for our kids.

I was thankful to have two strong hands to grasp those of my little ones in a place like Estonia, where everything and everyone was still in transition from the Soviet occupation. At times it was scary and stressful, particularly getting on and off public transportation with small children, but they were obedient and adaptive. Still so young, their daily routines were not so ingrained that they couldn't readily be changed. Their willingness to try unfamiliar foods, especially since I had to cook from scratch, made life easier for all of us.

With Estonia located so near the Arctic Circle and the North Pole, I like to say it is just south of Santa Claus. So, winters are long and dark, but during the summer months it is daylight for nearly 24 hours, the land of the midnight sun. This was a bit perplexing for the kids, wondering if it was day or night. I would try to darken the room where we slept, using towels or blankets to cover the windows, but their body clocks still got confused, almost like jet lag. Still, our children never complained. Just as my own mother had engendered a sense of safety and security in me because I trusted her, so Hannah and Caleb knew everything would be fine because we were together.

One day as we were walking around town exploring, I heard some pretty raucous noises coming from a huge, old, typically-gray Soviet building. Circling around it to find an entrance, I finally pulled open a door and walked into a large space occupied by several adults and children doing gymnastics. Although the outdated equipment was worn and torn, there were coaches working with kids on the various apparatus.

Approaching us, one of the Russian coaches who spoke some broken English explained that the gym was open every day and I could bring Hannah and Caleb to learn alongside the other children. Asking the price, I was amazed to hear it would only cost the equivalent of two U.S. dollars per month for both children, with unlimited use. Delighted to find a physical outlet for my energetic toddlers to let off some steam, we tried to go at least once a week, unless we were traveling to other parts of Estonia or into Russia.

Treating Hannah and Caleb with great kindness, the coaches let them follow the Estonian children, imitating their gymnastic routines. Despite the language barrier, the other children seemed to like having our kids join in with them, gently taking their hands and pulling them to the balance beam or the parallel bars to demonstrate a routine.

As time went on, I would learn that this Russian gym was actually run by the Mafia. Sometimes ignorance is bliss. But our appreciation for gymnastics continued even after returning to the States, where Hannah competed in the sport throughout high school.

As the months of 1993 sped along, the children would accompany me to the seminary when I taught a class, sitting contentedly in the back as they drew pictures or colored. When Wes taught, I would be with the children. I was always on the lookout for something new and different, something we could do together that would be fun.

With the Christmas holidays approaching, I started thinking of ways we might celebrate.

With such a dense forest behind our apartment, finding a tree was a good, simple start. Cutting down a little evergreen that wouldn't overwhelm our two simple rooms, we strung it with popcorn and construction paper cutouts the children had made. Eager to continue American traditions even while abroad, we wondered what to do about Santa Claus.

Most cultures have an iconic character who represents love and gift giving. Although we as Christians celebrate Christmas as the birth of Jesus, our secular cultural traditions include a jolly, white-haired and bearded, red-suited man called Santa. In Estonia, this figure is *Joulud*, meaning Old Yule; in Russia, he is known as *Ded Moroz*, Father Frost; in Finland, his name is *Joulupukki*.

Having been invited by the Methodist bishop to come to Finland for meetings in early December, Wes and I took the children on the ferry from Tallinn 30 miles across the sea to Helsinki. With signs all over the city enticing people to take a train to the Arctic Circle and visit the "home" of *Joulupukki*, I knew this might be the only opportunity we would ever have for such an excursion. Naturally, I was as excited as the kids.

Taking an all-night train up to Roveniemi, the four of us shared a tiny berth with two bunk beds. Entranced by the rapidly rising snow outside the train, I peered through the window with growing anticipation as we approached the station. Looking for all the world like a Hollywood movie set, it turned out that a crew had gathered there to film the reigning Miss Korea's visit to the Arctic Circle.

With such festivity in the air, we joined in the spirit of the season, first being whisked through the snow by a team of huskies on a sled, then riding in an open sleigh behind real reindeer! By the time 3 o'clock rolled around, it was already pitch dark outside, perfect for our visit to *Joulupukki*'s house. Living in a real town with real people, we discovered this Finnish Santa and Mrs. Claus also lived in a real house.

Before our audience with Santa would begin, we were led through a room where all his helpers, the elves, were busily at work. However, they were modern-day elves, about a hundred of them, typing away on computers in their signature elfin hats. The room, a cavernous warehouse, had as its focal point an enormous chalkboard where numbers were rapidly tallying the letters pouring in to Santa Claus from children all over the world. With our visit on the very first day of December, these industrious elves had already received a million letters addressed to *Santa, the North Pole*, and were actually answering them. Strewn with massive, letter-stuffed duffel bags, the elf room's atmosphere brought out the eager child in all of us, no matter our age.

At long last, we were invited to enter Santa's house, smelling like heaven on earth with the scent of cinnamon and spice floating through the air. The grandmotherly Mrs. Claus emerged from her kitchen bearing a cookie-laden tray, which she offered to each of us. After our yummy snack, we were led into a cozy room, what Americans would call a den or family room. And there he was—Santa Claus.

Having joined forces with an Italian family we had met earlier in the day, their little six-year-old girl was the first in line for Santa. Unfortunately, she was suddenly overcome by shyness and began sobbing, gripping her papa's leg as she hid her face from Santa's kind gaze and rather overwhelming beard. Her poor parents were not at all happy. I could just about see their brains reeling as they calculated the time and expense invested in this futile trip to the North Pole.

But Santa, being not only jolly but wise, asked what country they were from. Upon hearing "Italy," he immediately said, *"Buon giorno, piccolo ragazza!"* and continued to speak to the little girl in what sounded to us like fluent Italian. She instantly stopped crying and fell into Santa's welcome embrace, just like in the movie, *Miracle on 34th Street*. Laughing and chattering away, we couldn't understand what they were saying, but joy filled the air.

Then it was our turn, with no hesitation on the part of Hannah and Caleb. Jumping on Santa's knees, our kids began jabbering away. When he asked where they were from, little Caleb quickly said, "Russia," because we had just returned from ministering in Russia. So, Santa immediately began speaking to them in Russian. But big sister Hannah was not going to accept a partial truth, and added, "But we live in Estonia."

With that, our very versatile Santa Claus switched to rapid-fire Estonian.

Our mouths agape with astonishment, Wes and I exchanged looks of wonder. Deciding to playfully push the envelope a bit, Wes jumped in, saying, "Well, Santa, we do live in Estonia right now, but you can probably tell from our accents that we are actually from the United States.

"What state?" asked Santa.

As soon as he heard "Georgia," he thoughtfully put a finger alongside his nose, pondering his response before saying, "Ah, Georgia . . . home of Jimmy Carter, Coca Cola, and peanuts!" With that, we felt like we had stumbled across the REAL Santa Claus!

When our work in Estonia was finished, God led us into another new season, with a vision for training indigenous Christian leaders in their own countries. These leaders would in turn train others, whether from a tribe, village, or city, in their own language, multiplying the gospel in what we hoped would be an exponential way. Drawing on the contacts we had made through friends and in our travels to other countries, we began to connect with people around the world to test the viability of this vision that would become known as International Leadership Institute.

In the midst of the ILI birthing process and toddler stage, I continued to home school Hannah and Caleb, thankful for an option that enabled us to take them with us as we established a new ministry around the world. At ease interacting with those from different cultures and languages, our kids seemed to thrive on learning to communicate with others different from themselves, especially those less fortunate, like orphans.

Deeply thankful for the partner churches and individuals who have undergirded all our ministry efforts through prayer and financial support, they also helped keep our children safe and happy through their faithful prayers, letters, and care packages. As a missionary momma, I could not be more grateful.

What began in the year 2000 with a launch event in Amsterdam was followed by ILI's first international conference in November, 2001. Each successive year had brought unprecedented growth. At the writing of this book, there are more than 960 training events each year, with over 300,000 alumni across the globe in more than 100 countries. With gifted teams of leaders under regional directors around the world to organize training events, Wes and I continue to enjoy leading ILI and teaching in various conferences.

How marvelous it has been to see the hand of the Lord creating such a magnificent tapestry as we move in obedience to the Holy Spirit. To quote the late Corrie ten Boom, "It is not my ability, but my response to God's ability, that counts." Amen to that.

~

Oh, the depth of the riches of the wisdom and knowledge of God! How unsearchable His judgments, and His paths beyond tracing out!   ROMANS 11:33, NIV

Joy's parents,
Edward and Marie Smith
and brother, Kenneth

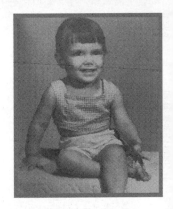

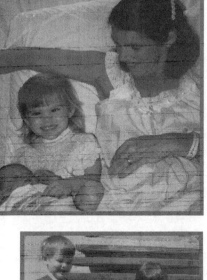

Blackie & Whitey

Russian Orthodox Church

*Our little Christmas tree
with homemade decorations*

Snow

*Hannah and Caleb at train station
sitting on the books for the seminary
brought back from Russia*

Hannah and Caleb in Zambia

*Hannah and Caleb
at Indian Springs*

Hannah peeling potatoes with her African friend

Ghana

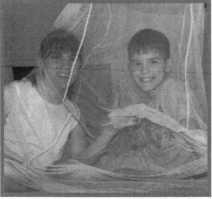

*Hannah and Caleb
in mosquito nets*

*Caleb playing
games with
the children*

India

*Joy teaching
the children*

Cricket

Kenya

*Widows
and their
first cow*

*The Strong Tower home
in Kenya with the
Operation Beautiful
Feet youth and the
former street boys who
now live in the home*

*Children at
the orphanage*

Turkana Women

Turkana Hut

Joy backpacking the Great Wall

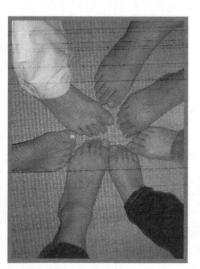

*Feet of underground believers
(cannot show faces)*

Man who was blind but now can see (holding hands with joy).

Jungle hut

Baptism

Maasai Tribe

*Ostrich egg
was my
thank you
gift*

Nigeria

India

Mideast

Samburu

*Jugs lined up
for pumping
water in a
refugee camp*

Dedicating hogs in Congo church

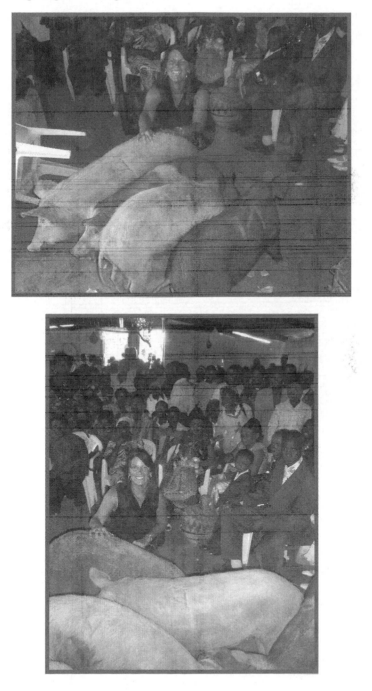

Prison Ministry

Ministry to pygmies and their beautiful feet
ready to share the Gospel with others

Joy and her Malaysian brother, Jih Ren. Teaching in Indonesia.

Burmese refugees in Thailand

Painting by Hannah Griffin

"...and you shall be My witnesses both in Jerusalem, and in all Judea and Samaria, and even to the remotest part of the earth." Acts 1:8

JOY TO THE WORLD

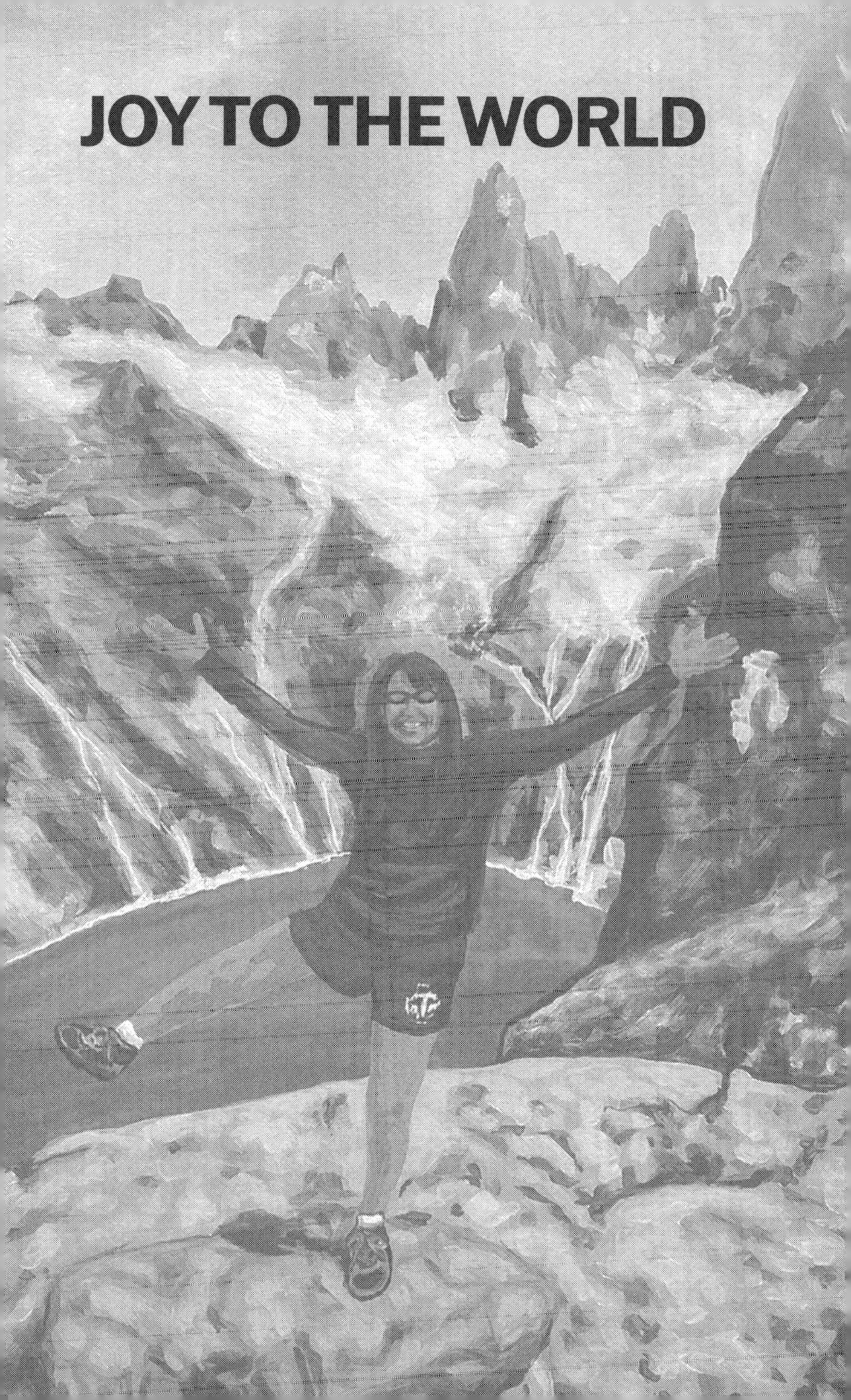

JOY TO THE WORLD—
AMAZON JUNGLE

"Anyone who believes in me may come and drink!
For the Scriptures declare, 'Rivers of living water
will flow from his heart.'"   JOHN 7:38, NLT

"THIS RIVER IS OUR LIFE."

Unspoken, yet undeniably implied, these words played out before me as I stepped gingerly onto the banks of the Amazon River in northern Peru. Having been deposited on the edge of the tropical rainforest by John, our missionary pilot, my friend Carolyn and I disembarked from the tiny, four-seat floatplane, our backpacks most likely representing more material goods than the sum total of all these precious Ashantika natives.

With some clad in rags and others in altogether nothing, young mothers were washing their little ones in the murky, dark-brown river water, while others were gathering the same in clay jugs for cooking. Young men in primitive dugout canoes were playfully splashing makeshift fishing poles in the muddy waters, angling for some piranha protein for their day's diet. Careful to respect their privacy, we trudged on through the rainforest to our camp, a thatched roof structure surrounded by a canopy of lush green vegetation.

Reflecting on my own life's journey that led up to this moment, my thoughts drifted several decades back to Christian camp meetings in my home state of Georgia. Every summer, my hardworking, dairy-farming parents would set aside a week to take my brother and me to a gathering with other believers for some good old-time revival meetings, fellowship around the campfire, singing gospel songs, and just plain fun. Having given my life to Jesus at the age of twelve, I was curious about going deeper in my walk with Him.

The next summer, I seized my opportunity. The missionary guest speaker had just shared a midweek message about all the unreached people groups of the world. "Did you know that there are parts of the world where people have never even heard the name of Jesus, much less been told the Good News? If you are feeling the tug of the Holy Spirit on your heart tonight to go to the unreached people of the world, to the uttermost ends of the earth, I invite you to come forward now."

Completely unaware of anything except that I was hearing Jesus call me to go forward, I leapt out of my seat and fell before Him on that sawdust-covered floor. "Here I am, Jesus. Send me!" As I prayed to receive this commission, I had a strong visual impression of a jungle rainforest. Somehow, I knew I would see it one day.

Now in the Amazon jungle, my childhood vision having just become a reality, joy exploded within me as I tearfully offered thanksgiving to God. "Thank you, Jesus, for answering my prayer! Even if you were to send me back home right now, you have fulfilled my dream! With all my heart, I want these people to know you!" Energized by my own elation, knowing that God had sent me and would be with me, I knew I could do anything through the strength Jesus would provide.

Equipped for foreign missionary service through my studies at Asbury Seminary, it was there I had met my friend and present travel companion, Carolyn. As a missionary kid raised in Guyana, she had longed to return to the South American rainforest of her upbringing, so she readily accepted my invitation to go to Peru. While my husband Wes was, and is, completely supportive of my many mission endeavors, the city boy in him preferred to sit this one out. "You go and I'll pray," he said.

So here we were! Knowing that our journey would have taken seven days by motor boat from Pulcallpa, I expressed my thanks to our pilot, John, and asked him to tell us what had prompted him to become a missionary pilot. Raised in Ecuador, John's Christian parents had become friends with now-legendary missionaries Nate Saint and Jim Elliot as they were attempting to evangelize the Huaorani Indians, a small, ferocious, unreached people group in the Ecuadorian jungle. Although Nate Saint and Jim Elliot were martyred when the Huaorani attacked and speared them to death, John's parents were in another location when this tragedy occurred. Hearing the story of these missionaries' selfless courage, John was determined to follow in their footsteps and went to the States to study aviation, eventually returning to his roots in South America. And now, John was helping us to spread the gospel here in the Amazon jungle.

Having been asked to speak at an evening service which other villages had been invited to attend, I was preparing my heart to listen to what the Lord had for me to share. Noticing some commotion around the compound, I saw a giant rodent the size of a small dog, something called *capybaras* in the Ashantika language, but which qualified as a rat in my book. Yet the natives were not fending this creature off; they were preparing him to be the main course for their evening meal! As the men dug a deep pit, threw in hot rocks from the fire, added Mr. Rat and smothered everything with banana leaves to keep in the moisture, I realized this would be my supper, too.

But there would be another delicacy on the table. A carb staple in the Ashantika tribe's diet is *yuka*, a form of the cassava root, which they dig up with machetes and then relentlessly pound into submission. However, this root is so hard that in order to make it edible, everyone is given a piece to chew on until it softens. And then . . . oh, Lord have mercy . . . they spit it back into a common pot for all to enjoy. Our evening meal would be Rat 'n Root.

Silently thanking God for all the ways He had prepared me for situations like this, I thought gratefully of one of my favorite professors at Asbury, J.T. Seamands, who taught us the importance of cultural relevance in missions. Wes and I, along with the other founders of ILI, included Culturally Relevant Evangelism as one of the eight core values of the Christian faith in ILI training. This basically means when in Rome, do as the Romans do. When in the Amazon jungle, eat rats and roots. And smile. Big. However, I did ask Jesus to help me not vomit as I swallowed it.

My upbringing on a dairy farm also did away with any squeamishness over sleeping on cow-manure floors, eating maggots and bugs like I did in India, drinking cow's blood in parts of Africa, you name it. I realized early on that not only my acceptance of native practices, but my participation in them, would build a bridge of trust between us. I would no longer be considered an outsider, but would become like one of them. I knew this was a key to being able to effectively share the gospel.

With just one precious hour to call my own between our afternoon teaching sessions and the evening feast and service at which I'd be speaking, I decided to take a dugout canoe out on the river and talk to Jesus, since He's always in the boat. But this one was pretty cramped, since a dugout is just a log with a big hole dug out in the middle where you sit. Grabbing a stick to serve as a paddle, I plopped down into the hole and shoved off from the shore.

"Jesus, the rest of the world doesn't even know these people are here. But you do, and now I do. They're unreached because it's so hard to get to them, so I want this time to matter for eternity. I want them to know you like I know you, Jesus. Tell me what to say to them tonight."

SPLASH! Suddenly, I heard a major disturbance in the water from the side of the river where I'd just been. Pretty sure it wasn't the Loch Ness monster, I still had a sense of imminent danger lurking in the muddy brown water, although its opaque darkness provided the perpetrator with a worthy disguise. Knowing I couldn't turn the dugout around too quickly or I'd capsize, I also knew Jesus was in my boat and would protect me.

"BOA! BOA!" Frenzied shouts from the natives on the river bank accompanied a geyser-like eruption from the water in the place I had just passed over. A giant, stone-gray creature was rolling violently behind me—a massive anaconda! This species of snake, a type of boa constrictor, can swallow a human being whole. In fact, anacondas in India are called "cow killers," because they can literally consume a cow in a single gulp. Having seen my shadow, this humongous serpent had surfaced to make me his evening meal, but somehow Jesus kept it at bay as He guided me safely to shore.

Resounding screams erupted from those who had witnessed it from the bank of the river. Having heard stories of friends and relatives who had canoed down the river to trade bananas and never returned, my close encounter with the anaconda overwhelmed them. Not aware that this danger was so present in the river that was life to them, that provided them with water to drink as well as for cooking and bathing, they quickly became aware that I had been protected from harm in a way that could only be described as supernatural. A somber sense of awe settled over the village that night.

With the dawning of the next day came bright sunshine and an excitement in the atmosphere as I prepared to teach. Wanting to share with the students about spiritual warfare from I Peter 5:8, I began to recite that verse, knowing my awesome interpreter, Carlos, would be working with me hand in glove.

"Be alert and of sober mind. Your enemy the devil prowls around like a roaring lion . . ."

Panic suddenly clouded the countenance of my very competent interpreter.

"Carlos, what's wrong?" I asked in alarm.

"There is no word in Ashantika for lion! I can't describe something that doesn't even exist for them!"

"Then just say 'big cat!'" I said.

"But we don't have cats either!" he said in exasperation.

Knowing we were between a rock and a hard place, I sent a quick bullet prayer to Jesus. Immediately, the answer came.

"Your enemy the devil is like a BOA! When he sees a shadow come over the water, he tries to drown it!" With that, the Holy Spirit connected all the dots, teaching these people that, while their river may be the source of their physical water supply, only Jesus can save them forever and provide the living water that will never run dry.

News travels fast, even in the jungle, but I was still surprised to see an array of multicolored native headdresses worn by several different tribal chieftains as they floated on boats down the river, coming to a stop at our village.

"We heard that God saved the missionary from the boa! We want to know about this God!"

Hallelujah! This opened the door for us to talk about Jesus being the Living Water.

Touched by the truth of God's Word coupled with this vivid testimony of His ability to rescue us from harm, many prayed to receive Jesus that evening, surrendering their lives to Him. Our prayers for the salvation of these people were answered.

Preparing for our departure to the States, we waited for John to return with the floatplane, eager to share these adventures with our pilot friend. However, the look on his face told us we wouldn't be returning to civilization anytime soon.

"I hate to tell you this, but there is a national strike in Peru of all the copper and salt mine workers. All transportation has stopped and there are armed guards everywhere.

But knowing you ladies and your call to share the gospel, this might be an opportunity for you to reach another group that has never heard about Jesus. It's about a 45-minute flight from here; the only thing is, I'm not sure we have enough fuel to get there and back."

Excited by the possibility, Carolyn and I agreed to go if there was enough. Climbing up on the wing, John stuck a dipstick in the tank. "I think I have enough," was the dubious verdict. While I'd have preferred something just a little more affirming, I figured it was worth a try.

"Promise me this, John," I said. "If you take us, when you return, stay along the river so you can land on the water if you need to!"

Agreed on that point, we took off for an even more remote part of the jungle. As we approached the area where John needed to land, he said, "We really need to pray. There may be people, goats, and who knows what else in the water, and then we can't land. So be prepared to jump out of the plane and I'll throw your bags out so I can keep the plane moving."

As we made our debuts as stunt artists, the people on the banks stared at us, two wacko white women wearing skirts and jumping out of an airplane! But the love of Jesus speaks a universal language, and we were able to share the good news with yet another unreached people group.

Our faithful pilot John was not able to make it back to retrieve Carolyn and me, so we had to devise some other way to get ourselves back to Lima. With the strike wreaking havoc throughout Peru, I knew we would have to find a driver who was willing to take some risks. Having reserved a hundred USD for emergencies, I figured this definitely qualified as one and paid a man to drive us through the cold, dark night through an area known for bandits.

Given the state of these jungle roads, if you can even call them that, it was not surprising when our vehicle broke an axle and came to an abrupt halt. Helping our driver hoist it onto a rock for a makeshift repair, he was able to at least get the car to move again, albeit at the pace of a tortoise. Limping along in the pitch-black night, we came across another disabled vehicle, a truck that had gone off the one lane pig-trail of a road and plunged into a ravine. Some questionable-looking men surrounded it and leered at us as we slowly ambled by. Although we had nothing valuable for them to steal, our nervous driver was quickly convinced of the power of prayer.

With daybreak, we crested a hill and caught our first glimpse of Lima! Pressing on towards the airport, we were surprised to not encounter any road blocks or guards, and soon learned that the Peruvian government had lifted strike sanctions earlier that morning. Sleepless, hungry, filthy, and yet somehow altogether elated, we heaved ourselves into our airplane seats and thanked God for seeing us safely on our way home. It was only after takeoff that we learned the strike had just resumed.

~

For He will command His angels concerning you to guard you in all your ways; they will lift you up in their hands, so that you will not strike your foot against a stone. You will tread on the lion and the cobra; you will trample the great lion and the serpent. "Because he loves me," says the Lord, "I will rescue him; I will protect him, for he acknowledges my name. He will call on me and I will answer him; I will be with him in trouble, I will deliver him and honor him. With long life I will satisfy him and show him my salvation."

PSALM 91:11-16, NIV

JOY TO THE WORLD—
THE VISA

Blessed are those who are persecuted for righteousness' sake, for theirs is the kingdom of heaven.   MATTHEW 5:10, NKJV

"Joy, now is the time you must come! We have only until the middle of June, when the Taliban will enact Sharia law as the official law of our country. If you can get here before then, it will be much safer for you. Otherwise, there will likely be many more bombings and terrorism."

The urgency in Asif's voice on a chilly January day several years ago caused my nerve endings to bristle with anxiety. The plight of my Christian brother in a persecuted country on the other side of the world fueled my desire to get to this nation before it became an impossible dream. Even now, for the sake of his security, I must tell this story without disclosing either his name or the nation in which he lives. A mighty man of God, Asif has been a key player in bringing Jesus to a country where Christianity is cursed, and has served as an integral part of our ministry. I wanted with everything in me to be able to accommodate his request.

Quickly processing the information he was sharing, I responded, "Asif, you know I'd love to come and teach; the problem is, I'm about to leave for Uganda right now, so I can't surrender my passport at this point to get a visa. Both of our kids will be graduating from college this spring, one in April and one in May, so I couldn't come to you until late May. Would that work for you?"

Agreeing that the tail end of May would still be viable for my visit, Asif and I made a tentative plan. On returning from Africa, I immediately sent my passport to the embassy of Asif's country in Washington, D.C., along with an application for a visa. Weeks rolled by, and then tallied up to months. I was not shy about badgering the embassy with inquiries about the status of my application, but continually met with either no response at all or a very terse, "No, your visa has been denied."

"Will you please tell me who I'm speaking with so I can call again?" I asked. Over and over, I would hear some variation of, "No, that's none of your concern." Every person to whom I spoke was extremely rude and not willing to be of help. Things were looking pretty impossible.

By then, it was nearly the end of May and my flight was due to depart from the States at 10 p.m. on the Sunday evening before Memorial Day, always the last Monday in the month. Still without either my passport or a visa on the Thursday prior to my scheduled departure, I phoned the embassy for the umpteenth time and was told, as with every time previously, that a visa had been denied.

Recognizing the voice of a younger man with whom I had spoken before, I appealed to his human decency, begging, "Please, please help me! Please don't hang up on me!"

After a pregnant pause, he finally said, "Okay, I'm just going to level with you. The truth is, we know all about you and you are very dangerous to our country."

"No, no! I just want to help your country!" I said. "How could I possibly be dangerous?"

"You're very dangerous spiritually," he admitted.

Deep in my heart, I was rejoicing, thinking, "I'm so glad they're afraid of me because of Jesus!" But that still wasn't helping me get the visa. My next thought was, *If they will approve it and overnight it to me, I can still leave on Sunday!* But when nothing had transpired by 6:00 Friday evening, I called Asif and resignedly reported, "We'll just have to postpone, because I still have no passport and no visa."

"NO! You MUST come, Joy! The time is NOW! You are like Esther in the Bible. The people have come as far as 2,000 kilometers for this—we are just waiting for YOU! You must go and get your passport back." Having lived all his life in a persecuted country, Asif knew how to persevere by faith. He wasn't taking no for an answer.

"Asif, it's not that easy. I've done everything possible. We'll pray . . . but I don't know what else to do."

Routine life goes on, even in the midst of a crisis, so I preached at a church that Sunday, grabbed a quick lunch, and got on the phone to the airlines, ready to try Plan B. "Here's my situation," I said to the agent. "I need to change my flight from tonight to Tuesday night instead. Can you do that for me?"

"Yes, Ma'am, that is possible. However, it will cost an additional $3,600 in addition to the $2,000 you've already paid for your present ticket."

Staggered by the thought of that monumental expense, I said, "No, I'm afraid I can't pay that. I was hoping you'd be able to do it for free."

"No, Ma'am, I'm sorry, but we are not able to do that." Click.

Hoping for a possible loophole with another agent, I called the same number again, asking the same question— and getting the same answer. Maybe the third time would bring a breakthrough.

Deciding to just spill everything up front, I said to Agent #3, "Sir, I don't know if you're a believer in Jesus Christ, or if you would even understand my story, but here it is. I have been asked to speak at a conference in a country where Christians are persecuted for their faith. I haven't yet been granted a visa, and my passport is being held at the embassy in Washington, D.C. I desperately need to change my ticket from tonight to Tuesday. That way, I can hopefully get my passport and visa from the embassy, fly out Tuesday night, and get there to teach and preach for at least part of this conference that all these people are counting on me for! Please, please help me!"

Hearing the percussive click of his keyboard, I was encouraged that he hadn't just said, "I'm sorry, but I can't do that," like the others. After a moment, he sighed and said, "Well, I really don't know why I'm doing this for you; I've never done anything like it before. But here you go."

So now I had a seat across the ocean, but still no documents to get out of the USA and into another country. Finally able to fall asleep in the wee hours of the morning,

I was interrupted at 2:30 a.m. Monday by a phone call from Asif on the other side of the world.

"Joy, are you on your way?" he asked.

Groggily, I answered, "No, I'm sleeping."

Asif reported that he had driven all night long to the capital of his country to ask officials to approve my visa, but they refused. We brainstormed some more.

"Maybe I could fly to Washington and go directly to the embassy and just wait there until they give it to me!" I said. There seemed to be no other recourse. I would just have to do it.

Calling the airlines well before daybreak, I asked if I could buy a ticket to Washington, D.C., from Atlanta. "Well, Ma'am, with the Memorial Day holiday, everyone is trying to get to the Capital for the ceremonies and parades. But it looks like we still have one seat left at 9 a.m."

My brain a bit fuzzy from lack of sleep, I said, "Well, let me think a minute," to which he interjected, "Ma'am, you don't have time to think because that ticket will be gone. It is literally the only seat left for the entire day!"

"Okay, I'll take it!" My fate sealed, I paid for the ticket and started stuffing my clothes into a travel bag. After driving to the airport and rushing through the check-in process, I was finally able to relax a little after boarding the plane. Despite the jam-packed flight, my thoughts drifted to the holiday we were commemorating. Memorial Day was indeed a bittersweet time for remembering those like my daddy, a World War II veteran, who had fought for us all so we would not have to give up our freedom. Realizing I was headed for a persecuted country where there were dictators and no freedom to speak of, I silently thanked God for blessing me with my American heritage.

Disembarking at the airport and arranging for a hotel in the city, I went to bed early in order to make it to the embassy by 7 o'clock the next morning. Knowing it would be expedient to appear culturally appropriate, I dressed in black from head to toe, similar to how the women would dress in the country of my destination. When the security guards unlocked the massive embassy doors, I entered the building and stood in front of a glass enclosure where passports and visas were processed.

"My name is Joy Griffin and I've come for my passport and visa," I calmly announced, although I felt anything but calm. Truthfully, I was quaking in my boots, knowing I was completely at their mercy.

The clerk quickly retrieved what appeared to be my passport, placing it under the glass.

"But where is my visa?" I asked.

"It has been denied," was the answer I had heard one too many times before.

Leaving my passport exactly where it was on the counter behind the glass, I pleaded with the clerk. "Please, you must help me! Will you please find someone who will give me my visa?"

Told by the clerk to wait, I sat in that stone-cold embassy all morning, observing other people coming in and out. It soon became apparent that no one was being granted a visa; the others were natives of this persecuted country now residing in the States, and their country of origin did not want them to be able to return.

As the hands rounded the face of the embassy clock and met at the top of the hour, I would get up from my perch and check to see if I had been approved. I knew Jesus would not let me down, because He wanted me to get there even more than Asif did!

At 1 p.m., a very tall man with an intimidating countenance stepped from behind a screen and announced, "Everyone must now leave the building. You may return at 3:00 and we will make our decisions then." Everyone complied but me. I marched up to him and said, "Sir, please help me! I have nowhere to go and no transportation. I'm begging you to let me stay here. I'll even sit on the floor if you'll let me stay until 3:00."

With my rationale being that if I left that building, I might never get back in, I persisted in standing my ground. At last, he resignedly nodded his head in assent, knowing I would not relent. As the man locked me into the embassy, I suddenly felt very alone in the dark, cavernous place.

As I waited, I once again called the airlines to try to change my 4:00 p.m. departure from Washington to Atlanta, sensing the unlikelihood of being granted my passport and visa in time to catch that flight. But with all the people who had come to the D.C. war memorials to commemorate the holiday, the next available flight wouldn't be until 8:45 p.m., which would make it impossible for me to be able to get on the 10:00 p.m. international flight. I had no option other than to give up my confirmed seat on the 4 o'clock flight and take the one at 8:45. I figured I'd cross the next bridge if and when I got my visa.

At 2:05, I was startled by this same tall man emerging from behind a wall in the shadows, motioning with his index finger for me to come over. Jumping up, I said, "Are they going to give me my visa?" He said nothing, but simply removed some papers from his coat pocket and said quietly, "Fill these out now. And sign this."

Writing as fast as I possibly could, I asked excitedly, "Are they going to help me?" But he never responded. When I finally finished filling out all the forms, he took something else out of his coat pocket—an American passport. My passport! Opening it up, he signed it, stamped it with the official seal, handed it to me, and urgently whispered, "You must leave here very quickly!"

As he unlocked the heavy door, I fleetingly wondered who on earth this man might be, but didn't waste any time in speculation. I made a beeline for the front steps, thinking somebody might be getting ready to take aim at my back. Totally disoriented, not having any idea where I was, I ran and ran, putting distance between myself and any danger lurking behind. I kept on running, so very relieved to have gotten my documents and to be on my way! Finally flagging down a taxi on Constitution Avenue, I asked the driver to take me to the airport.

Glancing at my watch, I suddenly realized with a twinge of excitement that there were exactly ten minutes before the 4:00 p.m. flight on which I was originally booked was scheduled for takeoff. Holding out hope while racing through the airport with all my might, I skidded to an abrupt halt at the gate, nearly colliding with a long queue of businessmen vying for seats on this overbooked flight to

Atlanta. Excusing myself as I cut through the line, I made my way to the gate agent and explained my situation.

"You have to understand, Ma'am, that this plane is overbooked; there are 27 people on standby. You are number 28," she explained.

Standing there amidst all of these competitive, angry-looking businessmen vying for a seat, I watched as the last confirmed passenger walked through the jetway and the door was closed. "Jesus, what do I do now?" I prayed. He had helped me all this way—changed my international ticket at no cost, provided the last seat from Atlanta to Washington, D.C., gotten me a visa against all odds—and now this? Somehow, I knew He would help me, I just couldn't imagine how.

Even as I was talking to Him right there in the middle of the crowd, I glanced up and saw the door to the jetway suddenly open a crack. The gate agent motioned towards me with her index finger, and all the men started charging in her direction.

"NO!" she shouted. "That woman!"

"Me?!" I said, my voice strident with surprise.

She nodded vigorously and motioned for me to hurry. Slipping quickly through the door, I waited as she slammed it with finality and turned to look at me.

Flinging her arms out in the shape of a cross, she said breathlessly, "What I just did is totally illegal. I've never done anything like this before. But we are going to walk down this jetway, and when we get to the plane, if there is an open seat, I'm going to give it to you. But if there isn't, you will have to make your way back through that mob alone."

Thanking her with all my heart, I knew Jesus had a seat for me, but the plane sure looked full. A flight attendant walked all the way down one side of the plane and came back to report that her side was completely occupied. Checking the other aisle, another flight attendant returned a moment later, exclaiming, "There is one seat at the very back of the plane!" *Thank you, Jesus!*

With all my ducks now safely in a row, I was able to make every connection and arrive in the country of my destination without any further mishaps. Met at the airport by contacts Asif had arranged, they also supplied clothes for me so I would fit in with the indigenous women there. Taken by car to a secret hideout in a building arranged for the conference, I was overwhelmed by the number of believers who had risked their lives to come together and worship Jesus.

"This is like heaven for us!" they said. "We are so encouraged to know there are so many other followers of Jesus in different parts of our country!"

We had to be extremely cautious and vigilant, and even had to relocate the conference midway through because it looked as if the officials had found us out. Still, God provided a huge tent in another remote location where hundreds of people were happily crammed in, sitting cross-legged on the floor. Men were on one side, women on the other, and children in yet another area, typical of this culture.

Although the conference had originally been planned for women only, limited to just 60 participants, the numbers had mushroomed and men wanted to be included as well. Within just six months of this first event, our initial training was multiplied to include over a thousand people, despite a complete lack of material resources.

Finishing the conference on June 8, I was able to return safely to Atlanta. However, four days later, just as Asif had told me might happen several months before, the airport was bombed and dozens of lives were lost. Terrorism has continued in this beleaguered country ever since.

Yet we take heart, knowing Jesus Himself opened doors for me that man had firmly shut. He made a way for hundreds of hungry believers to come together in worship, fellowship, and discipleship training that has been multiplied many times over. He has steadfastly protected Asif, his family, and all those working with him to spread the gospel in a hostile land. God desires that none should perish, and He is using every willing vessel to carry His love to a world that needs Jesus. What a privilege it is to be part of His kingdom on earth.

~

Blessed are you when men hate you, and when they exclude you, and revile you, and cast out your name as evil, for the Son of Man's sake. Rejoice in that day and leap for joy! For indeed your reward is great in heaven, for in like manner their fathers did to the prophets. LUKE 6:22-23, NKJV

JOY TO THE WORLD—
PING

God, who made the world and everything in it, since
He is Lord of heaven and earth, does not dwell in
temples made with hands. Nor is He worshiped with
men's hands, as though He needed anything, since
He gives to all life, breath, and all things. And He has
made from one blood every nation of man to dwell
on all the face of the earth, and has determined
their preappointed times and the boundaries of their
dwellings, so that they should seek the Lord, in the
hope that they might grope for Him and find Him,
though He is not far from each one of us.

ACTS 17:24-27, NKJV

HAVING PRAYED FOR MANY YEARS for an opportunity to
minister in mainland China, I finally resigned myself to the
reality that I might have to take a somewhat unorthodox
approach. Most of us are aware that in 1949, "Chairman
Mao" Zedong formed the People's Republic of China.
Mao, a revolutionary Communist, immediately expelled
all Christian missionaries from the country. Thinking this
measure would completely annihilate Christianity, he had
no idea that God had a plan to turn what the enemy had
intended for evil into good.

After submitting my application for a visa to China, I began to familiarize myself with the geographic area of this behemoth land mass, covering 3,700,000 square miles and comprising nearly one-fifth of the world's population. With an astonishing fourteen nations sharing borders with China, including many of those -stan nations that are so hard to pronounce and even harder to spell, their collective population makes up nearly half the people of the world! With so many of these nations closed to Christian missionaries, we prayed fervently for a way to reach these beloved children of God.

Opportunity knocked through an invitation for me to be part of a prayer walk with a group of believers from another part of the world. The understanding was that we would backpack and camp along the Great Wall, praying silently and without ceasing, but agreeing to not speak aloud to others of our faith in Jesus or to share the gospel. In fact, I had to sign a paper pledging that I would not talk about any religious or governmental matters, with the penalty for disobedience being potential arrest, imprisonment, torture, and perhaps even death. Despite this rather ominous-sounding threat, I couldn't wait to set foot in what the Chinese call the Middle Kingdom, a country viewed traditionally by its people as the center of the civilized world.

Meeting my likeminded, Jesus-loving, intrepid travel companions in Shanghai, we began our Great Wall adventure on this ancient collection of not one, but many, short walls, traversing the hills on the southern border of the Mongolian plains. Although we barely made a dent in its total length of 5,500 miles (8,850 kilometers), our week-long backpacking trek found us occasionally crawling on our bellies like reptiles through dense, deep-green forests to access the top of the hills where the old, crumbled ruins of the Wall were found. Dating back to a few hundred years before the birth of Christ, the Great Wall was built by the emperor as a means of protecting his territories from invading Mongolians and Huns. We quickly discovered why it was so effective in keeping out invaders. It was not an excursion for the faint of heart.

No creature comforts were to be found along the way, so we became accustomed to pitching our little lightweight tents in the corner of some unsuspecting farmer's pasture or cornfield. Lugging only essentials on our backs, we zig-zagged up and down, silently praying as the Spirit led for these precious people to come to a saving knowledge of our Lord Jesus Christ.

Although I was kind of bending the rules a smidge, sometimes in the evenings I would wander away from camp and visit families in their homes. Although we couldn't communicate verbally, I offered them the language of love, the language of Jesus. I smiled at them and talked about Him, knowing even if they couldn't understand my words, the Holy Spirit would be able to communicate the supernatural voice of God.

A primary goal of mine for this trip was to meet with some of the leaders of the underground church movement, as establishing face-to-face contact is essential in cultivating trust in the persecuted church. Letters, emails, and phone calls can be extremely dangerous forms of communication because others can report and turn you in, even years after initial contact. An entire church network can be wiped out in an instant, with brothers and sisters paying the dearest price of their lives.

With the help of the angels of the Lord working with some contacts I had, we were able to arrange a hush-hush meeting in a local park. Aware that the knots in the trees might have the eyes of spies behind them, we had to strive to appear inconspicuous. Still, the instant, joyful rapport of connecting with fellow believers transcended any apprehension of discovery. Reluctantly leaving my new-found brothers and sisters after our brief rendezvous, I blessed their beautiful feet to carry the gospel of peace to this nation so in need of knowing Jesus.

Knowing I would have to hightail it to the airport to make my flight, I hailed a *di shi* and jumped in. Greeting the middle-aged Chinese taxi driver, I asked his name. "Ping," was his one-word response. "Ping, my name is Joy and I'm from America. I'm so happy to meet you," I offered. Aware that anything I said could potentially be used against me, I waded carefully into the murky waters of conversation. *Lord, show me how to communicate with this man!* was my urgent prayer.

Although Ping's expertise in English was limited but definitely trumped my knowledge of Mandarin, I sensed the Lord prompting me to ask him what he believed. In response to my question, I received another one-word answer, "Nothing." Oh boy. That didn't help me one little bit. I prayed again, this time asking the Lord to open a door for me to walk through.

Drawing near to the airport, I realized my minutes were numbered and his eternal destiny was at stake. "Ping," I said, "what do you think happens to you when you die?"

He responded, "The government tells us that all Chinese go to the fire when they die." Suitably shocked, I wondered if I had heard him correctly. Not willing to risk being misunderstood, I persisted, asking the same question three times. With each repetition, his answer was the same. "All Chinese go to the fire."

Knowing that his response was scripturally accurate for those who die without knowing Jesus as their Savior, my heart raced with an urgent need to tell him about Jesus. "Oh, Ping—I don't want to be disrespectful of you or your government or anyone else, but I do want to tell you that God loves us so much that He has made it possible for you and me to not have to go to the fire!" My eyes blurry with tears, I watched his own narrow eyes widen with astonishment. Having never before heard the name of Jesus, the concept that there was a God of love was completely foreign to Ping.

"Ping, this God who loved the whole world so much that He gave His only Son, Jesus, to die in our place, to keep us from the fire—He wants for you to know He loves you, too. He wrote all about this in a big love letter, a book called the Bible. Have you ever heard of it?"

Shaking his head, Ping said, "No." Sensing he was cautiously receptive to hearing more, I added, "Ping, God says to us in that Book that if we search for Him with all our heart, we will find Him. So, I'm going to pray for you." To that, he responded in Mandarin, "*Xie xie*," which sounded to me like shay shay. But I knew he was saying, "Thank you!"

"I'm on my way back to my country now and I'm going to get this Book and send it to you. And it will be in your language!" I said excitedly.

"No," he said, holding up his hand in the universal sign language for stop. "It will never get to me. Communist officials go through everything and take what they do not want people to have."

"Well, I'm going to pray that God will get this Book to you. And when you do get it, I want you to read ALL of it!" I said, using my best school-teacher voice.

Fishing in my bag for a scrap of paper and a pen, I hastily scribbled out God's plan of salvation with supporting Scriptures: John 3:16-18; Romans 3:23 and 10:13; Acts 4:12; Ephesians 2:8-9. "While you're waiting for the Book, you can start with these," I added, handing him the paper just before climbing out of the cab.

Shoving the paper into his back pocket, he acknowledged it with a hasty "Xie xie," as we were now being watched by officials at the airport. Relieved that I had been able to at least plant a seed, I forged my way into the bustling terminal.

One of the first things I did on returning to the States was to order a Bible in Mandarin. Scouting around the house for a large box, I had the idea that bigger might be better when it came to disguising this precious cargo. Placing the Bible in the very bottom of the carton, I scrunched a bunch of old newspapers to look like trash, hoping the officials who opened it would just let it go as something very disinteresting.

And then I had another idea, certainly inspired by the Holy Spirit, a thought that really tickled me. I would take the box to a local Chinese restaurant and ask the owners to address the label for me so it would appear to be authentically Chinese and not English. They were delighted to conspire with me, forming the Mandarin characters with Ping's name and address, and handing back the box with an almost reverent sense of helping to fulfill a plan for their unknown brother on the other side of the world.

Having sent off the box with a prayer that it would reach its destination, I continued to pray fervently for Ping for weeks, and then months. You never know when you're just a prayer away from an answer, so I felt compelled to persevere. And then one day, an envelope arrived with my name on it, but no return address.

"Dear Joy," the letter began, "I received the package. I am reading the Book with great interest. I have many questions. Thank you. Ping."

"Glory to Jesus!" I shouted, probably loud enough for most of the state of Georgia to take note. I just knew our great God would get His Book into the hands of that precious seeker on the other side of the world. Yet with that letter, my prayers did not stop. I have continued to pray that God would send someone with beautiful feet into that taxi so they can help explain the Word to Ping and perhaps invite him into a house church fellowship. I've been praying fervently for the Spirit of God to reveal Himself to Ping, however He chooses.

Ping reminds me of millions of other Chinese who have never had the opportunity to hear the gospel, and of millions more in other persecuted countries or isolated areas around the globe who have not yet heard the good news of God's plan of salvation through His Son, Jesus. They need someone with beautiful feet to bring the good news of salvation to them.

We as believers in Christ rejoice in God's promise in Romans 10:13 that says, *Everyone who calls on the name of the Lord will be saved.* YAY! Big praise! Yet the next two verses ask several negative questions: *But how can they call on Him if they've never believed? And how can they believe in Him if they've never heard? And how can they hear without someone preaching to them? And how can anyone preach unless they are sent?*

But the culminating verse quotes Isaiah 52:7 with, *How beautiful are the feet of those who bring the good news of the gospel of peace.* This doesn't apply only to those like me who shuttle around from country to country, telling people the good news about Jesus. This is for all of you who pray for people like me, who give sacrificially to enable us to travel to the ends of the earth, who labor for the "away team" as you tend to duties at home. Your feet are every bit as beautiful as mine, and I thank you for this with all my heart.

God wants to use every available pair of beautiful feet to tell the world about Him. My prayer has been for more and more beautiful feet to step into Ping's taxi and help him understand the wonderful truth about Jesus. My prayer is for all of our beautiful feet to minister to those as close as our next-door neighbor or the single mom across the street or the lonely widow down the road. My prayer is for us to touch the heart of the colleague in the next cubicle at work or the checkout clerk at the grocery store. My prayer is for beautiful feet to reach the kids on the ball field or at band practice or in the classroom.

Sometimes God needs beautiful feet to minister right here at home in our own Jerusalem, and sometimes in Judaea, and sometimes in Samaria. And certainly, always, to the uttermost ends of the earth.

~

How beautiful upon the mountains are the feet of him who brings good news, who proclaims peace, who brings glad tidings of good things, who proclaims salvation, who says to Zion, "Your God reigns!"

ISAIAH 52:7, NKJV

JOY TO THE WORLD—
THE TURKANA

And the King will answer and say to them, 'Assuredly
I say to you, inasmuch as you did it to one of the least
of these My brethren, you did it to Me.'

MATTHEW 25:40, NKJV

WITH MY HEART always drawn to the last, the least, and
the lost, I knew this special request from Africa had my
name on it. With ILI's strong presence in Nairobi, Kenya,
I have traveled there frequently and always look forward
to meeting with our leaders and participating in their conferences. But this particular time, I was thrilled to go to
the Turkana region, a remote place a few hundred miles
northwest of Nairobi, to minister to an unreached, semi-
nomadic people group in an area bordering Uganda, South
Sudan, and Ethiopia.

With the dubious reputation of being spear carriers who
are not afraid to use them, the Turkana people have appeared
to be hostile to outsiders, a seemingly forgotten society over-
looked by the world and left to fend for themselves. But Jesus
hadn't forgotten them and knew they needed someone to
go and tell them about Him. I was elated to answer the call
to minister to these unreached people. Accompanying me
would be a core group from our awesome team in Nairobi.

With the semi-arid climate not being conducive to an easy way of life, the Turkana people have learned to persevere through 120-degree heat, often hiking for hours, if not days, to find water for their families. With their homes built over a frame of domed branches covered by thatched palm fronds, the roofs are plastered with cow dung in the rainy season to protect the interior sand floors. A family of six might live in a single hut that is only five or six feet across. They depend on their livestock, including goats, camels, donkeys, and zebu (a kind of humped cattle) for meat, milk, and blood.

Arriving at a clearing in the tribal compound, I was greeted by women and children wearing colorful, woven clothing, and men bearing multi-purpose staves that they used to prod livestock as well as to help balance themselves when carrying heavy loads. Everyone sported shaved heads, so my long, straight hair was a bit of a wonder to them. Since there was no electricity, I knew I would have to speak loudly and rely completely on God's ability to communicate the message He wanted them to hear through my interpreter.

After the first couple of days, adjusting my teaching to accommodate their culture, using storytelling instead of PowerPoints and smiling a lot to overcome the inevitable awkwardness, it was evident the people were hungry for more of God. The participants approached me to ask if I might be willing to preach a crusade to which they would invite others in the area. Not knowing what their idea of a crusade might look like, but certainly willing to try, I agreed. The men hastily constructed a makeshift platform in an open area in the desert, and before we knew it, hundreds of people materialized before our eyes.

It's significant to note that this part of Kenya is largely dominated by Islam, in addition to the Turkana people having their own traditional tribal religion that is endemic to the social structure, inseparable from their culture. Appeasing ancestral spirits is how they believe they will find blessing in their lives. Compounded by the legalism inherent in Islam, I knew the only way to truly reach their hearts was with the name of Jesus.

Stepping up onto the rickety platform with my translator, I hadn't even opened my mouth to speak before he furtively pointed to an ominous-looking man standing about 200 feet away, shouting at the top of his lungs.

"I need to tell you what's happening," my translator said, with more than a little agitation. "That man is the *mullah,* the muslim priest, and he is telling the people to not listen to you! He is saying he is going to take you out!" Somehow, I knew he wasn't planning to take me out to dinner. More likely, he was going to *have* me for dinner!

Knowing this was all-out spiritual warfare, my flesh recoiled in fear, with my first thought being whether I would ever get to see my family again. But almost immediately, my next thought was of the prophet Elijah in I Kings 18 and his showdown with King Ahab and the 450 prophets of Baal and 400 prophets of Asherah at Mount Carmel. I knew with every fiber of my being that the same God who fought for Elijah would also fight for me.

"Lord Jesus, help me to say your name in front of these people! You promise us in your Word that whoever calls on the name of Jesus will be saved!" Although my prayer was silent, I felt as if my spirit was shouting with a megaphone all the way to heaven. Knowing that these people had never had access to the gospel or even heard the name of Jesus, I sensed the most important thing I could do would be to speak His name.

Talking in very short, distinct sentences, I forced myself to slow down my normal speech patterns. Even as my heart was about to burst out of my chest, I focused on listening to what the Holy Spirit was instructing me to do. Having previously shared with some of the conference participants the story of my miraculous healing from paralysis, I was asked to share that testimony with the crowd. Observing their rapt facial expressions as the interpreter translated my words from English into Swahili and then Swahili into Turkana, I felt sure I had their attention. The Holy Spirit was at work in their hearts.

Encouraged by such a visible response, I enthusiastically preached on with more and more excitement, getting to the point where I knew I should offer an invitation for them to receive Jesus as their Savior. Our group from Nairobi had previously agreed with me in prayer for at least one Turkana to be saved that night. They were prepared to go out into the crowd to pray with anyone who desired prayer after I spoke.

Approaching that critical moment, guess what Jesus did?! I suddenly noticed something curious out of the corner of my eye. The intimidating, angry *mullah* simply got up and walked away. I have no idea where he went, but his leaving seemed to shift the atmosphere in the crowd. A couple of hundred people edged forward, coming closer to me, as I invited them to receive Jesus as their Savior and Lord. But no one came forward like they would at a typical crusade to profess faith in Him. They just started pushing and shoving with a mob mentality like you'd see in a riot.

If Jesus weren't standing there with me, it would have been terrifying. Yet these people were not angry and aggressive; they were weeping and begging for healing. In a culture where there is no sanitation, poor dietary habits, and no medical care, these desperate people wanted what I had myself experienced—the healing touch of Jesus.

With hundreds flocking toward me, I had just barely prayed for one person before my translator got pulled away in the crowd, leaving me to fend for myself. Unable to communicate in their language, I just began laying my hands on two people at a time, either on their shoulders or their heads, praying for their salvation, praying for their healing.

Now deep into the crowd, surrounded by flailing hands trying to grasp me from every which way, I encountered for the very first time a woman who was possessed by demons. Banging her head in the dirt, growling like a rabid animal and foaming at the mouth, I was so startled by her actions that for a split second, I could only stare.

Suddenly, I recalled one of my former Asbury Seminary professors, J.T. Seamands, talking about demon possession from his vast missionary experience in India. As demonic manifestations are a frequent occurrence in that part of the world, he had explained, "A demon-possessed person cannot or will not say the name of Jesus. You simply plead the blood of Jesus over them, because only His blood can deliver them."

So, I dropped down on my knees in the dirt next to her and began praying as the Spirit led, oblivious to anything and everything else. As I prayed, I watched the power of the blood of Jesus transform this woman's countenance from one of crazed eyes rolled back in her head to complete, peaceful clarity, with her gaze squarely focused on me. And then this precious woman, still disheveled and covered in dirt, spoke to me in the Turkana language, *"Kiperoi Yesu!" Glory to Jesus!*

At the same moment Jesus was delivering the demoniac woman before our eyes, loud cheering was erupting from an area surrounding the platform. Looking up, I watched as an elderly Turkana man walked up to the makeshift stage by himself. Although that didn't seem all that unusual to me, what I didn't know at the time was that he was known as the village blind man, having been completely without sight for 20 years. A young man stepped up beside him, as if to demonstrate the authenticity of this healing, thrusting his hand out to the formerly blind man. As the onlookers gaped in amazement, the old man extended his hand, grasped the one offered to him, and shook it. The crowd roared its approval.

As the people were not literate, the old man's sight couldn't be further tested by giving him something to read, so the young man on the platform began to speak the name of someone in the large crowd and tell the old man to point to that person. He was able to flawlessly identify every one of them.

As I made my way back up to the platform, I said to the crowd, "It was Jesus, the God who loves you so much, who touched and healed this blind man! The god of Islam is empty and has no power. But Jesus is the strong one who wants to fight for you!"

I was a little puzzled that several people left at that moment and headed for their huts, as I hadn't quite finished. But soon they came back, bringing even more villagers with them. The good news of Jesus and His power to heal and deliver prompted the Turkana people to get the word out right then and there. Bringing everyone they knew who was sick, lame, or blind, they trusted Jesus to heal them. And He did.

I've never witnessed as many signs and wonders as I did that night. Another blind person, this one a woman, received her sight. A lame man using a crutch threw it to the ground and jubilantly ran around. The power of Jesus to heal and deliver was everywhere, His kingdom having come on earth as it is in heaven.

Now, every time the Turkana people see their fellow tribal members who were healed, they witness a living memorial to what Jesus has done among them. The old blind man, once relegated to a life of complete dependence on others, is out working in the village, living a productive life. The woman possessed by demons is able to function with a sound mind. Their lives now testify to the One who made them, the same One who saved them. *Kiperoi Yesu!*

And they overcame him (the enemy) by the blood
of the Lamb and by the word of their testimony,
and they did not love their lives to the death.

REVELATION 12:11, NKJV

JOY TO THE WORLD—
PRISONERS

"Then the righteous will answer Him, saying, 'Lord, when did we see You hungry and feed You, or thirsty and give You drink? When did we see You a stranger and take You in or naked and clothe You? Or when did we see You sick, or in prison, and come to You?' And the King will answer and say to them, 'Assuredly, I say to you, inasmuch as you did it to one of the least of these My brethren, you did it to Me.'"

MATTHEW 25:37-40, NKJV

IN THESE DAYS OF SOCIAL DISTANCING and increased isolation, it breaks my heart to think of those who are incarcerated, locked up within the walls of prisons, desperate for contact with the outside world. Jesus tells us in Luke 5:32, *"I have not come to call the righteous, but sinners, to repentance."* But how will they even have an opportunity to repent unless they are able to hear the truth that will set them free?

For this reason, it was such a privilege to be asked by our ILI colleague, David Thagana, to go with him to a maximum-security prison in the Aberdere Mountain region of Kenya. Although the building's capacity was only intended to house 300 men, there were a total of 800 prisoners living in that facility when we arrived.

While no prison I know of has ideal living conditions, this one was not only primitive, but barbaric. Entering the barbed-wire compound, manned by legions of guards with seriously intimidating guns, we were told that the prison population included 120 murderers, who were further isolated from the other inmates by a chicken wire fence. The remaining 680 men had been convicted of crimes like robbery, rape, kidnapping, forgery, and identity theft, the same as anywhere else.

None of the men wore real clothes, just tattered rags to cover their essential anatomy, and very few wore shoes. Personal hygiene was virtually nonexistent. They would line up for meager meals that consisted of a bowl of rice, or maybe water with a few green leaves that suggested soup. These men would sleep 80 to a room in cramped, filthy, smelly barracks. It was hard to imagine how anyone could stay alive in circumstances like these.

Amazingly, the chief warden in the main area of this prison was a believer in Jesus, so we were given the opportunity to preach to the prisoners as well as offer leadership classes. We told the men they would receive a graduation certificate if they attended every class. This was a huge incentive and honor for them, since many had never been able to attend school.

Eager to see what we might have to offer, the entire prison population of 800 men turned out, sitting cross-legged on the dusty ground. As we presented the good news of Jesus to them, the Holy Spirit pierced their hearts with His arrows of love, bringing tears of conviction and then genuine repentance. Many came forward at our invitation, confessing their sins and asking Jesus to forgive them and live in their hearts. What a glorious celebration of God's redeeming blood!

As some of the men shared their testimonies, one said, "I came in here a convicted felon. I was guilty, but now I know Jesus has forgiven me. When I leave this place, I will leave as a leader, and I'm going to share everything I've learned here with others."

These redeemed prisoners began to think of creative ways they could help encourage their fellow inmates, and some began dreaming of what they might be able to do when they were released. They talked about building a halfway house for former inmates, a place to learn a trade like gardening or tailoring. They began to believe they had hope and a future.

We were so excited to bless our new friends with gifts provided through donations from Operation Beautiful Feet. Our Nairobi team purchased used clothing, a shirt and pants, as well as a pair of rubber sandals, for each and every inmate. Packing enough to supply all 800 men, they loaded dozens of enormous black trash bags into the bed of an itty-bitty pickup truck. But before we could distribute them, every single bag had to go through the prison's primitive security system, basically meaning they had to be opened and searched. But finally everything was approved, and it was as if Christmas had come to that prison.

While some in Third World countries might look down their noses at such items, our men felt like royalty. And they were, sons of the King of kings and Lord of lords. We said to them, "This is for you from Jesus, just because

He loves you. He knows you are here, and He cares for you more than you can even imagine. He longs for you to love and live for Him."

Jesus is able to make even the hardest heart, the foulest life, clean and new. He doesn't leave us alone to figure it all out; He walks with us through every single thing we will ever face, and promises to use it all for our good when we love Him and are called to His ways.

~

See, I am doing a new thing! Now it springs up;
do you not perceive it? I am making a way in the
wilderness and streams In the wasteland.

ISAIAH 43:19, NIV

JOY TO THE WORLD—
ORPHANS

Religion that God our Father accepts as pure and faultless is this: to look after orphans and widows in their distress and to keep oneself from being polluted by the world.   JAMES 1:27, NIV

"Mzungu! Mzungu!" The excited cries of hordes of children accompanied our arrival in the town of Naivasha, Kenya, a 60-mile drive from Nairobi. This Bantu term for people of European extraction with Anglo-Saxon features was often accompanied by curious little hands reaching out to try and touch our milky-white skin. Would it feel the same as theirs? And what about our lighter colored, straight hair? Why were we wearing such strange looking clothes? And who in their right mind would put things on their feet?

Along with our children, Hannah and Caleb, Wes and I were on our first family mission trip to Kenya. Met by our friend and ILI colleague, David Thagana, we were thrilled to explore this magnificent country of astonishing natural beauty. At the same time, our eyes could barely process the depth of poverty staring us in the face from every vantage point.

Taking us to Naivasha, a large town of about 200,000 located northwest of Nairobi, David wanted to show us the most tragic consequence of the AIDS pandemic in his country—orphans. With Hannah being in the seventh grade and Caleb in the fifth, their young hearts were unprepared to see street urchins their own age and even younger, scavenging for anything that might possibly be edible. Wearing filthy rags, some of them had an object concealed under their tattered garments that appeared to be a bottle. Pulling it out every now and then, they would hold it up to their noses and sniff. Asking a medical doctor what this was all about, we were told it was glue the kids were sniffing to stave off their constant hunger pangs.

When we returned to America and our normal routine, I resumed teaching Hannah's and Caleb's Sunday school and VBS classes, alternating between the two each year. This particular year, I was on the Caleb rotation, teaching and discipling fifth graders. Being missions minded, I always liked to share something cultural with my class from a place where we had served.

Pulling out photos of the Naivasha orphans one Sunday morning, their reaction was the same as my own children when they had first seen these homeless, parentless street children. Shocked and deeply distressed, Caleb's classmates said, "Miss Joy, we've got to help them!"

"Well," I said, "let's start saving our money. If you will be diligent in studying God's Word, staying and praying together, we'll see how we can make a difference in these kids' lives. And when you get old enough, if your parents agree, I will take you there."

This group of 12 or 13 kids committed themselves to following my suggestion. Through middle school and junior high, and then even into high school, they stayed together and spurred one another on toward their common goal. When birthdays or Christmas rolled around, they would ask their parents and relatives for money to help the orphans in Africa.

To get their missional feet wet, I was able to take them on two trips to Mexico when they were young teens, fueling their zeal for taking Jesus to the nations. Designating themselves as Operation Beautiful Feet, these precious young people then joined forces with another local church group to buy land near Naivasha, Kenya. Their intent was to build an orphanage, a place where these homeless children would finally find a place to belong. I would have the great privilege of dedicating that building, along with a few other adults who came along to do medical missions and work with the kids.

The same little fifth-graders who had dared to dream big were now young men and women, juniors in high school. They had persevered toward their goal, working hard to save money, and the time had come for us all to go together to Kenya and see the fruit of our promise. Coming with me to Naivasha, they saw with their own eyes what God can do when we commit our ways to Him.

Seeing that first group of 23 boys now living as a family under one roof, our hearts were nearly bursting with gratitude to the Father of the fatherless. Although the facilities were pretty basic, with iron bunk beds in two or three tiers in the dormitory and no running water, these boys were so thankful to be safe and have their needs met. In fact, they decided to name their home Strong Tower, in acknowledgement of Proverbs 18:10, *The name of the Lord is a strong tower; the righteous run to it and are safe* (NKJV).

With a local woman, Jane, serving as Strong Tower's housemother, these boys were provided with nourishing, home-cooked meals and a stable foundation. Our team had been able to find individuals, families, and churches in the States to agree to sponsor the children for a year at a time, covering the cost of their living expenses as well as school tuition. We also brought along some school supplies and little seedlings to plant trees around the building.

What fun we had, playing volleyball and soccer with the kids, just doing what normal young people like to do. And since our little mission team was called Operation Beautiful Feet, we decided it would be fitting to take all the boys into town and buy them each a pair of shoes—their very first.

As our visit was coming to a close, I felt prompted to take all my Sunday School kids to the slums of Naivasha, the same place my family and I had first seen these orphans. Taking along some juice and crackers, along with a few other basic provisions, we shared what we had with the kids on the street. Having heard about the orphanage, those who were still homeless looked at us, their penetrating, deep brown eyes asking the inevitable question, *What about us?*

Just as they had done years before when I showed them the photos of the Naivasha orphans, our teens didn't miss a beat as they said, "Miss Joy, we've gotta do something!" As we prayed and planned, we felt led to construct another building up on the hill near Strong Tower.

Knowing this project would take many months, we enlisted the help of the street kids to do their part, urging them to be respectful and not harass the police. Giving them our word, we returned to America and the teens began raising funds to build a second home, this one for girls.

Now in its tenth year of operation, Strong Tower currently houses 65 children in an environment where they can blossom and flourish. The Lord has also provided them with cows, goats, and chickens to raise for milk, cheese, eggs, and meat, and they have planted gardens to raise vegetables to eat or barter for flour, oil, rice, and other staples. What began as the heart's desire of young children to help others less fortunate than themselves had come to fruition as we trusted not in our own ability, but in God's ability to provide for the needs of all His children.

~

He administers justice for the fatherless and the widow, and loves the stranger, giving him food and clothing.　　　　DEUTERONOMY 10:18, NKJV

JOY TO THE WORLD—
WIDOWS

The widow who is really in need and left all alone puts her hope in God and continues night and day to pray and to ask God for help.   I TIMOTHY 5:5, NIV

WHILE MINISTERING in several different areas of Kenya a few years ago, David Thagana approached me towards the end of my visit and said rather cryptically, "The widows are waiting for you." Looking for all the world as if he expected me to know what he meant, I figured something was lost in translation because I really didn't have a clue. What widows? And why would they be waiting for me? But because I know and trust David, I just assured him I was available and ready.

Hopping in his car to drive to the Kinangop region of Kenya, we arrived at a typical, Kenyan-style church in a community called Ndunyu Njeru. But instead of stopping there, David continued around the back to a dilapidated, much older structure. Entering through the rickety door, we found 15 women of various ages—all of them widows. And from the eager expressions on their faces, they had indeed been waiting for me. At least that part of the mystery was solved. But I still wasn't sure what Jesus wanted me to do for them.

As I asked these dear women some questions, trying to help them feel comfortable, encouraging them to open up, it became clear that each of them had walked quite a distance to get to this meeting. Apparently, a time had been arranged for the meeting I had not been aware of, and I began to feel the burden of responsibility for making it worth all the effort it took for them to get here. *Jesus, I need you. Show me how to love them for you during this time we have together.*

Looking out at their world-weary countenances, I felt His compassion welling up from deep within me. I noticed some were younger widows, probably still raising their children at home; others were grandmothers, taking responsibility for grandchildren whose parents had died. And some were more my age bracket, in between. But each one, despite ragged clothes and no shoes, was a princess daughter of King Jesus. And He began to show me what He wanted me to do and what He wanted me to say.

"I want to tell you about a group of five American missionary pilots who went to evangelize an unreached group of people in the jungles of Ecuador in the 1950's," I began. "Now, I've ministered in the Amazon jungle and it isn't always a friendly place because the people aren't used to outsiders. But in this case, a tribe of natives attacked these missionaries and speared them to death, leaving their wives widows with young children.

"I can't imagine how these women must have felt, hearing of the deaths of their husbands. But several years later, Elisabeth Elliot, the wife of pilot Jim Elliot, and Rachel Saint, the sister of pilot Nate Saint, returned to Ecuador to live as missionaries among the same tribe that killed their loved ones. Eventually, many members of that tribe received Jesus, including some of the murderers. They were able to see an entire culture transformed.

"I've also had the privilege of ministering in Congo, where a widow is often shunned by family members following the death of her husband. Ancient tribal customs cause women to feel degraded or even completely humiliated as they are forced to look down at the ground, speak only when necessary, and receive rations of food and water from relatives. Not allowed to bathe or comb their hair, they are forced to wear only certain types of clothing and pay the husband's burial expenses even when their material goods are being taken away from them. All these things are manipulative ways for women to be made to feel responsible for the deaths of their husbands.

"But there are many examples in history of bold, brave women who fought for what they believed and preached the gospel, even when it was not acceptable for women to do that. Although she was not a widow until the last five years of her life, Susanna Wesley, the mother of Methodist church founders John and Charles Wesley, persisted in following God's plan to proclaim the gospel, no matter the cost."

As they listened intently, absorbing these stories of courageous women who bucked what society dictated, I asked if they would be willing to share their stories with me. Gradually, as they began to participate in our group conversation, I learned they were all part of the same village, attending a church pastored by a 45-year-old man named Apollo. Married to a beautiful wife, having several children, Apollo worked hard at a vocational job during the day while pastoring this church the rest of the time.

With a deep compassion for widows and orphans, Apollo challenged the widowed members of his church to form a group to encourage one another, spurring each other on with creative ways to make a living. Accepting his challenge, the women formed a little club, with one of the younger members acting as secretary, keeping detailed minutes from each meeting in what was surely the rattiest little notebook I've ever seen.

Their original plan centered around pooling all their financial resources, with their goal being to purchase animals. However, among the 15 of them, their combined wealth amounted to 80 Kenyan shillings, equivalent at that time to 80 cents, not even one US dollar. But they were convinced this would work, and decided they would not buy a single animal until each of them could have their own. After a year of saving their money, these remarkable women had enough for each of them to buy a chicken, which would supply eggs for their families.

Bolstered by their initial success, they continued meeting and encouraging each other to save money. Five years later, they had enough for each one of them to buy a goat, which would provide milk and even some cheese. It was evident to me how excited they were to share their success stories with me, so I said, "I'm so proud of you! So what's next? How can I pray for you now?"

Like little kids anticipating Christmas, they said, "We want to buy a cow!" Now this could really be a big-time business venture for them. If they were able to purchase a cow, they would not only have milk for themselves, but potentially enough to sell at the market. They would be real businesswomen!

Feeling the undeniable prompting of the Holy Spirit, I prayed with them and sensed the Lord giving me a go-ahead to share what He was saying. "Ladies," I said, "I feel confident Jesus is going to provide you with a cow." Thinking of Beautiful Feet, the same group that has provided time and time again for needs like this around the world, I knew they would come through with resources to buy the first cow for these widows. Beside themselves with joy, singing exuberantly in their native tongue, jumping up and down, they all took turns hugging me.

The next step was for me to speak to Pastor Apollo, since he was their overseer. "Apollo, will you agree to be sort of like a surrogate husband to these widows and lead them through this process? Will you go and find a Holstein cow that is not only exceptionally strong, but pregnant? That way, when she freshens, they will be able to multiply." Remember, I grew up on a dairy farm, so I knew that cows only begin to give milk after they have given birth to a calf. I knew these women needed every advantage they could get.

Pastor Apollo worked with great diligence, trying to locate someone who was selling a cow. Since only wealthier people owned cows, he needed to find an individual who might be in a temporary financial pinch, needing to sell a cow to pay their kids' school tuition and fees or something. And that's exactly what happened.

A week after I boarded my plane to return home to Georgia, I opened our mail on that Saturday morning to find a most welcome photo. Surrounding a magnificent, very plump, black-and-white Holstein were 15 beaming widows! Pastor Apollo had bought the cow, led it by rope to these women, and taken a photo for me to share with the Beautiful Feet team who had helped to purchase it. And then, much to my amusement, they named the cow Joybells, after me!

I had promised the women I would return and prove to them that a white woman can milk a cow. While they found that hard to believe, I reassured them it was second nature to me. And I did eventually make good on my promise. Their plan was to share Joybells (the cow, that is) a week at a time, so she'd be moved every seven days to a different woman's little plot of land. That way, all would benefit from the fresh milk, if only for a week.

But guess what Jesus did? The same day Pastor Apollo brought them their cow, she went into labor and within 12 hours, delivered a precious little calf. God had given them a double portion, an answer to our prayers. He had multiplied this gift the very first day!

When I began sharing the story of the widows and the cow with local churches and Sunday school classes, suddenly everyone seemed to want to jump on the bandwagon (or maybe it was the hay wagon) and help to buy a cow. Then Tom, a dear brother in the Lord, died of cancer. His widow, my friend Jan, asked people to make contributions to Beautiful Feet as a memorial to her husband, rather than sending flowers. The next cow to join the widows' team was named Tomasina, in honor of Tom.

As others continued to raise money and contribute to the efforts of these widows over the next two years, it was thrilling to see them attain the fruition of their dreams. Every single one of these 15 widows is now the owner of her own cow. As these women share not only their cows' milk but their stories, they are able to witness to others of God's perfect provision. He is, after all, the owner of the cattle on a thousand hills.

"For all the animals of the forest are mine, and I own the cattle on a thousand hills. I know every bird on the mountains, and all the animals of the field are mine . . .

~

Make thankfulness your sacrifice to God, and keep the vows you made to the Most High. Then call on me when you are in trouble, and I will rescue you, and you will give me glory."   PSALM 50:10-11; 14-15, NLT

JOY TO THE WORLD—
REFUGEES

My God of my strength, in whom I will trust; My shield
and the horn of my salvation; My stronghold and my
refuge; My Savior, You save me from violence.

2 SAMUEL 22:3, NKJV

WE AS BELIEVERS IN JESUS know *it is for freedom that
Christ has set us free* (Galatians 5:1), but much of the
world has had to contend repeatedly for political as well
as spiritual freedom. With my first stop on this particular teaching mission being Liberia, I knew this beautiful
coastal country in West Africa was still suffering from the
effects of two civil wars over a period of about 23 years.
Still living largely without electricity, the people were
slowly beginning to emerge from poverty.

After preaching in a large church in the capital city
of Monrovia, I thought of how ironic life can sometimes
be. A country whose name means "free" and whose capital city was named after the fifth president of the United
States, James Monroe, Liberia was intended to be a refuge for U.S. slaves who had been set free. But there had
been decades, nearly two centuries, of division caused by
ethnic competition, governmental corruption, and economic inequities.

Like all of us, they needed Jesus. It was so gratifying to be able to teach to a sizable group of intentional believers who were determined to see their country transformed. I am confident they will, because Jesus is on and at their side.

Reluctantly leaving my new friends in Liberia, I headed for my next destination, South Sudan. However, the African continent is notoriously difficult to navigate, so I steeled myself for a zigzag journey that would take me from the west to the east coast in four flights. Although it seemed very counterintuitive to fly northwest to Sierra Leone, then back east across Liberia through Cote D'Ivoire into Ghana, that was my itinerary for the first two stops. Waiting for others to deplane and board, I warmed my seat for more hours than I'd like to remember, finally departing Ghana for Nairobi, Kenya, which is on the east coast of Africa.

With a layover of several hours in Nairobi, I was glad for a large terminal so I could stretch my legs before boarding my flight to South Sudan. But there were very few amenities to be found in the airport, so I focused on walking and talking with Jesus about what I would need for the days ahead. He is always faithful to clue me in on what I need to know. Finally, our flight boarded and I was on my last leg of a long day's journey.

South Sudan is the youngest independent country in Africa, having separated from Sudan in 2011 over division between Muslims in Sudan and non-Muslims in the southern region, now known as South Sudan. Although you might assume the conflict would be religious in nature, it really is a fight over natural resources like oil, gold, and other minerals.

With the separation came an upheaval in the infra-structure of South Sudan, which seemed to be almost nonexistent. Civil war raged between the sixty-some native tribes in South Sudan, rife with nepotism and corruption. One tribe seemed to be most prominent, dominating the others and creating a constant threat of danger.

Meeting my friend and colleague, David Thagana, to teach together, we were strictly instructed to not leave our building because of the lurking danger of kidnap-ping, rape, and murder. With corruption extending even to the police, you couldn't expect the long arm of the law to reach out and protect you. With such extreme poverty that the average person can't feed their family, theft was a common occurrence.

With such a tribal culture, the people had grown accus-tomed to living in fear, defending themselves by attacking others with machetes. We even saw little seven-year-old kids strutting around with machine guns, and they weren't toys, either. There appeared to be absolutely no rules and no sense of accountability.

David, a native of Kenya, felt even more insecure than I did because of the color of his skin and the growing con-sciousness that these people knew he was not one of them. But we had work to do there, and until Jesus returns, we must occupy and take the territory for His kingdom.

Leading our training sessions in a primitive, stifling-hot space, we soon discovered it was a constant challenge to fall asleep at night. My room, a tiny mud hut, had a token lock on the door, but both it and the door handle were broken, leaving a gap anyone could peer right through.

I guess it was probably good that it was pitch black at night, since without electricity, you couldn't even see your own hand in front of your face. My nocturnal companions were huge, slithering lizards and monstrous mosquitoes, with easy access to me through the opening in the hut. But at least I didn't see any snakes.

Despite the oppressive heat and lack of electricity, the Holy Spirit came powerfully as we taught these eager students. Staying inside a small building for the sake of safety, we observed several of the participants standing by themselves, maybe in a corner, praying out loud. Others would lie prostrate on the floor under a table, submitting themselves to the Lord in worship and prayer.

Just as I had finished preaching and given an invitation for them to surrender everything to Jesus and be filled with the Holy Spirit, something so sweet happened. As people came forward to receive prayer, suddenly a breeze came wafting through a little opening in the wall. I just knew it was the wind of the Holy Spirit. The breath of God was blowing so gently on each of us. What a gift.

David and I had planned to leave South Sudan immediately after our group graduation ceremony to drive several hours south to Uganda. South Sudan is bordered there by DR Congo, Uganda, and Kenya, and we were headed for a refugee camp at the northern tip of Uganda. Because South Sudan is notoriously dangerous, Ugandans do not live that far north, even though it is their country. But the Ugandan government has allowed hundreds of thousands of South Sudanese to set up tents or build mud huts in this remote desert territory.

After driving nine hours from South Sudan, David and I still had to cross the very deep and wide Nile River in order to reach the refugee camp. As we rode in our car on a ferry, my thoughts turned to the story of Moses and his sister Miriam in the book of Exodus. Although the Bible doesn't specifically name her as Miriam, we know the sister of Moses was a key player in arranging with Pharaoh's daughter for baby Moses to be cared for and nursed by his own mother.

"Lord Jesus," I prayed, "Would you raise up one of your people in this place to be a leader like Moses for these precious people?" I knew we had a wide-open door for effective ministry set before us, just as the apostle Paul says in I Corinthians 16:9. I also knew we had many adversaries, the chief among them having a job description to steal, kill, and destroy (John 10:10). But God promises He has come that we might have abundant life, and has given us His Holy Spirit as a deposit guaranteeing what is to come (2 Corinthians 1:22). Praise God for His indescribable gift.

Pulling into the refugee camp of some 200,000 South Sudanese, we were overwhelmed not only by the sheer number of makeshift tents, but also by the intensity of the desert heat. With all these people packed together like sardines, in scorching heat hovering between 110 and 120 degrees Fahrenheit, it seemed like a recipe for disaster.

We knew the people were in despair, wanting to return home but afraid to go, having no jobs, feeling isolated from civilization. The United Nations would bring in truckloads of maize and beans once a month, but supplies would dwindle within a week and disappear by the middle of the month. These people were hungry in every sense of the word.

As I lay in my tiny hut, praying for Jesus to touch these desperate souls, I was periodically distracted by little scratching, scuttling sounds on the dirt floor. With my cot just a foot above the ground, I knew it wouldn't be much of a challenge for critters to jump up and join me, so I flipped on my flashlight. The first thing I saw was a pack of rats running relay races around my cot, but then the ray of light illumined the reason they were running. A cobra.

Staring defiantly at me, his appearance defined by the characteristic cobra hood, I knew this guy was nothing to mess with. Now, I've killed snakes before, which I actually like to do because it makes me think of doing the devil in, but I had absolutely nothing to use for the job. No sharp or heavy objects of any kind were in that hut, not even a stick. I had actually helped beat another cobra to death earlier that day in the mud church we used as a classroom. But I had nothing now. I knew one of us was going to have to make an exit. And it would be me.

Knowing I had my Rope Holders interceding for me, I cried out, "Jesus, please tell somebody to pray!" Knowing He would give me what I needed, I ended up outside with my flashlight, standing out in the open for hours at a time, night after night. Since Sir Snake had slithered into the dirt in my hut, I knew it could be there waiting to crawl over me if I dared go back in there. But Jesus provided rest for my soul, even when my body was weary.

Living in the midst of all these dear, displaced people, God showed up in a mighty way. Walking among them, waiting with them as they stood in line, sometimes for many hours, for water they pumped by hand into any container they could find, we got to be Jesus to them. Most had never seen a white person before, so some were a bit afraid of me at first. Others wanted to touch my white skin and finger my long, straight hair. I was happy to make any kind of connection with them.

We had come equipped with gifts provided by Operation Beautiful Feet, not only food, but five manual sewing machines and some bolts of cloth. Among the countless indignities of living as a refugee was that women had no provisions to deal with their monthly periods. These gifts would enable them to sew little towels for that purpose.

God's Word tells us in Matthew 24:14, *And this gospel of the kingdom will be preached in all the world as a witness to all the nations, and then the end will come* (NKJV). We know there are still unreached people groups, and some remain unreached because it can be incredibly difficult to get to them. Even if you do, there are language barriers, cultural differences, physical dangers, and just plain creature discomforts.

But God goes before us and behind us, Jesus goes with us, and the Holy Spirit even interprets for us! There is no better place to be than in the center of His will.

~

You will trample upon lions and cobras; you will crush fierce lions and serpents under your feet! The Lord says, "I will rescue those who love me. I will protect

those who trust in my name. When they call on me,
I will answer; I will be with them in trouble. I will rescue
and honor them. I will reward them with a long life and
give them my salvation. PSALM 91:13-16, NLT

JOY TO THE WORLD—
RWANDA, CONGO, AND THE PYGMIES

Instead of your shame you will receive a double portion; and instead of disgrace you will rejoice in your inheritance. And so you will inherit a double portion in your land, and everlasting joy will be yours.

ISAIAH 61:7, NIV

I LOVE IT WHEN JESUS sends me to minister in Africa. My heart is so aligned with these beautiful people, living in a land so full of natural beauty and resources. Maybe because there are still so many unreached groups of people, I feel drawn to do as much as I can to share Jesus with them and see leaders effectively trained to multiply the gospel.

The tiny country of Rwanda, which is comparable in size to the state of Maryland, was our first stop on this teaching tour. With mountainous terrain and many lakes, it has the greatest population density of any country on the mainland of Africa. Although Rwandans come from just one primary cultural heritage, the Banyarwanda, there are three subgroups within that designation: the Hutu, Tutsi, and Twa, also known as the Pygmy people.

Rwanda is unfortunately best known for the horrific genocide which took place between April 6 and July 16,

1994, in the midst of what was already a civil war. Beginning in 1990, a longstanding rivalry between the Hutu and Tutsi ethnic groups erupted into a full-scale battle. The presidents of Rwanda and Burundi, both of the Hutu tribe, were returning to the presidential palace in the Rwandan capital of Kigali when their airplane was shot down by surface-to-air missiles. Both men were killed, plunging Rwanda into utter mayhem.

At the end of the 100-day killing spree, some 800,000 people were killed by retaliating Hutu extremists, with the majority of those slain belonging to the Tutsi ethnic group. In the midst of the slaughtering, up to half a million women were viciously raped, with more than two-thirds of them contracting HIV and eventually AIDS. With countless children left as orphans, many tried to hide in the dense forests for weeks and even months, attempting to make it to the border of one of the neighboring countries, especially nearby Burundi.

I found myself wondering how the Hutu extremists knew who their opposition, the Tutsis, were if both tribes were from the same cultural heritage. But I learned there are distinct physical differences between the two tribes, with the Tutsis being taller and lighter-skinned, having long, slender noses. The Tutsis primarily raised cattle, while the Hutus were more involved in farming the land. But they still shared the same language and culture, and everyone in the villages knew each other. I was horrified to hear about Hutu radicals going from door to door during the 100 days of atrocity, and if they recognized a Tutsi, would slash them to death with a machete.

With about 75% of the Tutsi population murdered, the country was still in an understandable upheaval when we arrived, trying desperately to rebuild. Accompanying me on this trip was a colleague from Kenya, so we were able to ask many questions of those we were teaching in the conference. Even though my Kenyan friend was living in a country only about 800 miles from Rwanda, she had never even heard about this genocide, although the horrific news had traveled quickly to the United States.

As we toured the Kigali Genocide Memorial, I saw countless telegrams sent from Rwanda to various world capitals like London, Rome, and Washington, D.C., begging for assistance. The world seemed to be clueless, unaware or even uncaring that some 8,000 people were savagely losing their lives each day. It was truly a holocaust, but was perceived by outsiders as tribal warfare. It seemed as though no one wanted to get their hands dirty by interfering.

Since Wes, the children, and I had been living in Estonia in 1994, we had no knowledge of this tragic event until years later. And now I was here to minister to those who had suffered beyond comprehension. Our conference hosts took us to a mass burial site in Kigali to view the graves, telling me at one point that there were 250,000 people buried beneath our feet. Even today, over a quarter-century later, it is not uncommon for people to find human bones in the fields or forests.

As my Kenyan colleague and I ministered to the pastors, youth ministers, and business people attending the conference, a huge part of what we accomplished that week was to just listen to their stories and try to help them heal. Every woman I met while in Rwanda had been raped and tortured—and these were the ones who had survived. Many were maimed and disfigured by the violent acts committed against them.

Many churches arose from this egregious genocide, several of them with names like Restoration Church or Church of Restoration. God promises to restore the years the locusts have eaten (Joel 2:25), to bring beauty from ashes, gladness for mourning, a garment of praise instead of a spirit of despair (Isaiah 61:3). He sees these beautiful, recovering people of Rwanda as oaks of righteousness, a planting of the Lord for the display of His splendor. He Himself will restore them, making them strong, firm and steadfast (I Peter 5:10).

* * *

Deep in the heart of the African continent, the Democratic Republic of Congo was our next destination. Also known as Congo-Kinshasa to differentiate from its cousin to the west, the Republic of the Congo-Brazzaville, the DR Congo is a large, landlocked country. Surrounded by nine other nations, to the north are the Central African Republic and South Sudan; to the east are Uganda, Rwanda, Burundi, and Tanzania; to the south are Zambia and Angola; to the west, Congo-Brazzaville. DR Congo is the second-largest African nation in land area, after Algeria.

Traveling into the eastern side of Congo, the pastors there had requested our ILI leadership training as well as for me to preach in their churches. You need to know that sometimes this just meant gathering with a group of people under a tree, as there were no formal facilities or audio-visual enhancements. But Jesus always showed up, and that's when church is really church.

The various pastors spoke to me about ministering to particular groups of people, like women who had been raped. They also asked us to go into the jungle to the Pygmies, a group very marginalized by society. I had no idea what to expect, but knew Jesus would be with us and the Holy Spirit would provide the counsel and comfort they needed.

One Sunday morning, I had preached in a church where the majority of women were dressed nicely in their Sunday best, wearing colorful, long dresses or skirts. Following the service, I was taken to a dark part of the building on the opposite side, where another group of women awaited me. *Desolate* might be the best word to describe the looks on their faces. Eyeing me cautiously as I straddled one of the packed-mud benches to sit among them, these women acted as if they felt unworthy of even being seen or heard. Were they ever in for a surprise.

My interpreter explained that all of the women had been victims of rape in a country where rape was considered a weapon of war and no man was held accountable for it. Even law enforcement officers could not be trusted to protect the women. With decades of inequality, oppression, violence, and governmental chaos, rape had not only destroyed individuals, but negatively impacted the entire culture.

Coinciding with the Rwandan genocide, there was an increase in the number of rapes in Congo. Some of this was attributed to Hutu radicals taking refuge in Congo, as well as fighting for control over land and mineral rights. Added to this was the ridiculous cultural superstition/misconception that rape was empowering. During the times of civil unrest in Rwanda, Burundi, and Congo, rebels would move through a town after pillaging and murdering the citizens, with military generals claiming the territory and "rewarding" their men by leaving them to do as they pleased.

With zero accountability and no consequences for such heinous acts, it was not uncommon for a pre-pubescent girl, young woman, or even an older woman to be serially gang-raped over and over again, even to the point of death. At times, parts of their bodies were brutally mutilated or even bitten off. Ears or breasts might be cut off with machetes.

In Congo, the women who had been raped became like the untouchables in India, complete outcasts from society. No one would give them a job or rent a room to them. Their children were not allowed to go to school because they were a product of rape.

Even among the Congolese who attended church, there was a stigma against women who had been raped, seeing them as defiled. Despite being victims who had done nothing wrong, they were treated as pariahs, not welcome to interact with mainstream society, even within the church.

As I surveyed the desolate women around me, my heart was overwhelmed with sorrow. Nothing had prepared me for this. *Holy Spirit, I need your help. I need you to show me how to comfort them. I need you right now!*

There are times in life when words can't touch pain—but tears can. As I sat and wept with these precious ones,

I let the liquid love of Jesus flow through me. After a while, I said, "I have never experienced what you have. But I do know our God is a loving God and He longs to bring restoration to your hearts and healing to your bodies. You are worth everything to Him. You are a princess daughter of the King of kings! Even if the devil has tried to strip you of your value on this earth, Jesus has come to restore it."

Sharing with them the story of my miraculous healing from paralysis, I explained how God longs for us to be made holy and whole, desiring to fill us with His Holy Spirit. As I promised to pray for them, I went around the circle to each woman. Holding out my arms, I embraced each of them for a long, long time. Our tears mingled as they melted in my arms. The Holy Spirit was meeting each one with the love of Jesus.

As I was preparing to leave, I glanced across the room to see the well-dressed ladies of the church huddled in a corner on the other side of the room, watching with more than a little curiosity. Raising my voice so they could hear, I turned to them and said, "My sisters, you should be the first example of love to these sisters. I challenge you to pray about letting them rent a room in your house, or helping them find a job. Maybe you could help their children be able to go to school."

Well, the Holy Spirit came over that place with power, convicting every heart. Suddenly, the ladies in their Sunday best came over to join the women in rags, beginning to warmly hug and talk with them. Since that day, I have been told they have made a considerable effort to help their sisters on the other side.

● ● ●

Our final stop on this particular tour was deep in the forest jungle of Congo to minister to the Pygmies. Comprising only about two percent of the population of Congo, they have been ostracized from society, marginalized because they are different and therefore misunderstood. Characterized physically by very short stature, with adult males less than five feet tall, they have been feared by others because of their animistic beliefs and savagery. Most governments have forgotten them, not considering these people equal to others.

Taking with us some Congolese church members who had actually been afraid of the Pygmies, I shared Jesus with all of them. "Jesus wants to love you and give you your self-worth, regardless of what men or governments may say. He made you in His image and He has a plan to prosper your life and give you hope for the future." As the Holy Spirit moved among us, God's word penetrated their hearts, and they were changed.

Moved by what the Holy Spirit did for his tribe, the chief offered me a truly unique gift of thanks—the full headdress of a tribal chieftain. But this wasn't an ordinary, feathered headdress; it was the full skin of a leopard—body, legs, and head. Fortunately, the innards had been removed. Humbled by the honor of this gift, I squatted down before the chief as he placed it on my head. Although I couldn't quite explain to him that I wouldn't be able to transport his gift back to my country, the blessing of his intention will forever remain a gift to me.

As these precious Pygmies came to Jesus, drawn by His loving acceptance, some were baptized, and I believe all felt His love. The Congolese church members accompanying us began to see their hearts were no different from the hearts of their brothers and sisters, and a spirit of unity came into our midst. Reconciliation had begun with the love of Jesus.

~

All this is from God, who reconciled us to Himself through Christ and gave us the ministry of reconciliation: that God was reconciling the world to Himself in Christ, not counting people's sins against them. And He has committed to us the message of reconciliation. We are therefore Christ's ambassadors, as though God were making His appeal through us.

2 CORINTHIANS 5:18-20, NIV

JOY TO THE WORLD—
EVERY NATION AND TRIBE

For if the blood of bulls and goats and the ashes of
a heifer, sprinkling the unclean, sanctifies for the
purifying of the flesh, how much more shall the blood
of Christ, who through the eternal Spirit offered
Himself without spot to God, cleanse your conscience
from dead works to serve the living God?

HEBREWS 9:13-14, NKJV

Y'ALL KNOW I'M A GEORGIA GIRL, no secret about that.
Everything I am and do reflects my upbringing there, and
I'm very proud of it. As a citizen of the United States of
America, I love my country and all its fifty states, but I'm
particularly fond of Georgia because it's my cultural heritage. Yes, I'm an American through and through, but I relate
to the culture—the food, customs, wildlife, vegetation, idi-
omatic expressions—of my state of Georgia much more
than I would to that of New York or Minnesota or Oregon.

We often misconceptualize other parts of the world
by thinking the inhabitants of a certain geographic area
all look, think, and act like one other. Nothing could be
further from the truth. Having had the opportunity to
serve as a missionary in 21 of the 54 African nations, I
can unequivocally say each nation has a distinctly different

"flavor" and the people are as marvelously unique as those within our fifty United States.

Just as we Americans are accustomed to regional variations in accent, style of dress, recreational preference, architecture, and cuisine, so the people of Africa—and certainly every other nation—also reflect a diverse spectrum. Not only is each country distinctly different from the ones around it, but within its borders, there is also a tribal uniqueness. With some 3,000 tribes represented among the 1.3 billion inhabitants of the African continent, diversity is a given.

I've been fascinated for years by the Maasai tribe, a nomadic people found in the East African regions of Kenya and Tanzania, tending to live along the Great Rift Valley. It sounds almost like an oxymoron, but the Maasai are pastoral warriors, making their living primarily by raising cattle and, when necessary, killing others for them. Believing the cow to be sacred, entrusted to them by their deity called Ngai, the mark of a successful Maasai tribesman would be a large herd of cows and a hutful of children.

Elegant in stature, standing tall and thin, the Maasai love dressing in vibrant colors, especially in red. Because it is the color of blood, they believe it is sacred, and also helps protect them from wild animals. Because they live far from civilization, the Maasai plant acacia trees to fence in the tribal compound in an effort to keep the big cats—cheetahs, leopards, and lions—outside. A night watchman keeps a fire burning to further discourage predators.

Since their huts are made from cow manure, and the cow is considered holy, women and children actually fight over daily cow droppings. Having slept inside a Maasai hut, I can reliably say it's not easy to breathe in there, nor can you see a doggone thing. Sleeping on a cowskin on the cow-manure floor, I wasn't sure whether I'd prefer to see what life form was sharing my bed or not. It isn't unusual for baby cows to share a hut with their human family. Of course, this means more cow manure and everything that goes along with it. Typically, the Maasai stay in one location for five to seven years. When the wood sticks supporting the cow manure huts begin to rot from termites, it's time for the tribe to move on.

With their reverence for cows, perhaps it's only natural for them to drink cow's blood, but it certainly was not natural for me. Although they eat beef sparingly, blood is an excellent source of protein and the cow does not need to be killed to get it. The Maasai simply stick them in the neck and drain the blood. Naturally, all eyes were on me to see if I would dare to be like one of them. Asking Jesus to help me not vomit, I took a swig and smiled. As I passed the test, they all cheered. In my heart, however, I desperately wanted them to understand the power of the blood of Jesus, the only acceptable sacrifice for our sins.

One of the most disturbing customs practiced by the Maasai involves circumcision as a rite of passage, for both males and females. In the center of the cow lot, the place where the cattle spend their nights, is a long pole cut from the limb of a tree. Known as the circumcision pole, a 16-year-old male is strapped to it with his arms wrapped around the pole as the witch doctor or *shaman* cuts and removes the foreskin with what is usually a rusty, filthy machete. Then the young man is sent out into the wild bush alone, not to return home until he kills a lion and brings back the head and mane. Once this proof of manhood is presented, he can take a wife.

Women are not highly valued in the Maasai culture, so girls are not allowed to get an education and are repressed by the male-dominated society. When a young woman reaches puberty, her female genitalia is cut with a machete, robbing her of any potential physical pleasure in married life. This barbaric practice sometimes causes young women to acquire a life-threatening infection or even to bleed to death. Tragically, it occurs in many different cultures and tribal territories around the world. I have heard the ominous drumbeats accompanying horrific screams of pain as the bodies of young women are wickedly violated. I pray for this atrocious, inhumane practice to come to an end.

A monotheistic culture, the Maasai believe their god Ngai has a dual nature, both benevolent and vengeful. Steeped in animism, they are a difficult tribe to evangelize. Central to their religious practice is the *laibon*, a kind of soothsayer whose role traditionally includes healing, divination of spirits, and foretelling the future. They are highly regarded in the tribal community for guidance in many areas of life.

A few years ago, I traveled a substantial distance with my Kenyan brother, David, to teach and preach in a Maasai village. Just as we always pray will happen, Jesus touched the heart of the village chief and he received Him as his Savior and Lord. This presented a serious dilemma for the *laibon* as the chief began to be transformed before everyone's eyes. Suddenly, the village chief wanted to talk about Jesus and pray to Him, not consult the *laibon*.

Witchcraft went out the window as the chief began to treat his wife and family differently. He urged his 50-year-old wife, the mother of his five children, to begin to attend school. She started learning the alphabet right along with their youngest child. Real transformation was taking place as this tribal influencer now began to influence for the gospel.

As a symbol of the chief's genuine gratitude to David and me, he presented us with priceless gifts—a goat for David, and a beautifully decorated ostrich egg for me. The ladies had noticed a freshly-laid egg outside my mud hut one morning, quickly retrieved it, and added lovely multi-colored beads as their gift of gratitude to me. David and I were delighted to return the following year to continue our ministry to these precious people.

Ten months later, we were asked to go to another village to dedicate a new church. The original group we had been privileged to serve were so excited by the salvation of their chief that they became believers and then went to another Maasai village to evangelize the tribe there. The process of multiplication took place as they shared what they had learned and experienced with those who had never heard the Good News. As that new church was dedicated, we celebrated together with a huge feast, eating roast goat meat and, of course, drinking cow's blood. But what was becoming apparent to these people is that only the blood of Jesus, the Lamb of God, cleanses us of all unrighteousness. *His blood can make the foulest clean, His blood availed for me.*

These words of Methodist hymn writer Charles Wesley from *O for a Thousand Tongues to Sing* speak of the power of the blood of Jesus to redeem everyone who calls on His name. As no respecter of persons, Jesus offers Himself to every tribe and every nation, to all who call upon His name.

O for a thousand tongues to sing my great Redeemer's
    praise,
The glories of my God and King, the triumphs of
    His grace!
My gracious Master and my God, assist me to
    proclaim,
To spread thro' all the earth abroad the honors of
    your name.
Jesus! the name that charms our fears, that bids our
    sorrows cease,
'Tis music in the sinner's ears, 'tis life and health
    and peace.
He breaks the power of cancelled sin, He sets the
    prisoner free;
His blood can make the foulest clean; His blood
    availed for me.
To God all glory, praise, and love be now and
    ever given
By saints below and saints above, the Church in
    earth and heaven.

The Spirit of God is moving throughout the whole, wide earth, hovering in places where many of us will never go. But we can all be part of what He is doing by joining our hearts as one Body and one Spirit, one Lord, one faith, one baptism, one God and Father of all, who is above all and through all and in all (Ephesians 4:4-5). Whether we go ourselves or help to send others to these faraway places, interceding for them as they go, we work together to bring Jesus to the world. We will only know when we get to heaven the wonders God has wrought in response to the prayers of the faithful.

~

After these things I looked, and behold, a great multitude which no one could number, of all nations, tribes, peoples, and tongues, standing before the throne and before the Lamb, clothed with white robes, with palm branches in their hands, and crying out with a loud voice, saying, "Salvation belongs to our God who sits on the throne, and to the Lamb!"

REVELATION 7:9-10, NKJV

JOY TO THE WORLD—
BENEDICTION

Still others had trial of mockings and scourgings, yes, and of chains and imprisonment. They were stoned, they were sawn in two, were tempted, were slain with the sword. They wandered about in sheepskins and goatskins, being destitute, afflicted, tormented— of whom the world was not worthy. They wandered in deserts and mountains, in dens and caves of the earth.

And all these, having obtained a good testimony through faith, did not receive the promise, God having provided something better for us, that they should not be made perfect apart from us.   HEBREWS 11:36-40, NKJV

THE ELEVENTH CHAPTER of the book of Hebrews, often referred to as the Hall of Faith, chronicles men and women who were willing to be used by God in sacrificial ways, even to the point of death. From the patriarchs who lived before the Flood, to the tribes of Israel brought forth from the seed of Abraham; from Moses leading the Israelites out of Egypt to Joshua bringing down the walls of Jericho; from the harlot Rahab to the judges and the prophets, we read of those lives *of whom the world was not worthy* (Hebrews 11:38).

And then we see God's perfect plan revealed before our eyes— Jesus as the fulfillment of the New Covenant, *the author and finisher of our faith* (Hebrews 12:2). We who are alive now are running the race set before us, keeping our eyes on Jesus. We are inspired not only by the great cloud of witnesses named in the Hall of Faith, but by our present-day brothers and sisters around the world who are likewise offering their lives as living sacrifices. The world is not worthy of them.

How blessed I have been to meet and minister with so many brothers and sisters living in closed-access countries, where anyone professing faith in Jesus can count on being persecuted and perhaps even martyred. Searching for safe hideouts from which to teach and preach, hearing bombs explode in a building next to our meeting place, having to be rushed by vehicles under cover of night to another location when security has been breached, huddling as a group in the dark corner of a room so as not to be seen through windows by outsiders—I have sipped from the bitter cup of persecution along with these fellow followers of Jesus. Yet they must remain, drinking daily from that cup, while I live in a land where I can still openly worship Him.

While the overt persecution of Christians around the world is outrageous in any form, there is another kind of danger lurking in a less obvious way, particularly in the Western world. With much of our contemporary Christian heritage originating in Western Europe, there is an encroaching spiritual void where secularism has overtaken the souls of the people in the very places where the gospel once spread like wildfire. Places like Greece, Italy, Germany, and England, where denominations were established and the Church flourished, are now seeing their magnificent cathedrals reduced to mausoleum-like museums. Yet there is a devoted remnant, passionately continuing to spread the gospel.

In Eastern Europe, whose republics were once part of the U.S.S.R., liberation from Communist occupation opened the door to political freedom, but many spiritual obstacles remain. Along with the positive aspects of democracy, negative doors were also opened to outside influences of pornography, drug addiction, alcoholism, crime, and apathy. But faithful young people, the children and grandchildren of those who had lived under Soviet occupation, are making an enormous impact as they choose to commit their lives to being leaders of leaders under our Lord Jesus Christ. What a privilege it is to teach and preach there, encouraging them to multiply what they are taught.

Still other parts of the world where I have served, particularly in the Middle East, South America, areas of the Caribbean, and the Asia Pacific region, must remain unidentified. Any mention of the work we are doing there would potentially endanger the participants. But these brave followers are relentlessly willing and eager to receive training and tools to multiply the gospel, knowing it is the only hope we have for our world. Despite being marginalized, almost physically fenced in to their environment, their souls are free in Christ, and they are free indeed! The world may never hear of them, but our Father in heaven knows their names and has written them in His book of life.

Throughout the Bible, God urges us to remember what He has done, to teach His ways to our children, and proclaim His faithfulness to all generations. In sharing these stories of encounters with the Holy Spirit through ministry around the world, my intent has been to give you a glimpse of some of the amazing things Jesus has done by recounting some of my own experiences. I bless you to share them with others and to go forth and make disciples, wherever God has planted you. I urge you to continue to pray for all who serve the Lord, even as I thank God for my personal Rope Holders whose prayers have protected my family and me through every danger, toil, and snare.

As I conclude this book, the most fitting way is with the words which end the gospel of John.

~

This is the disciple who testifies to these things and who wrote them down. We know that his testimony is true. Jesus did many other things as well. If every one of them were written down, I suppose that even the whole world would not have room for the books that would be written. JOHN 21:24-25, NIV

Jan de Chambrier & Joy Smith Griffin

JOY SMITH GRIFFIN

Joy co-founded the International Leadership Institute (ILI) in 1998 to change history by accelerating the spread of the life-transforming power of the Gospel through leaders of leaders empowered by the Holy Spirit. Today, over 300,000 alumni serve on the cutting edge of Christian leadership in more than 108 nations. ILI's unique contribution is the discovery of the Eight Core Values of the most effective Christian leaders. Around the world, over 900 training events are held annually. For more information go to www.ILITeam.org.

Joy is an internationally-acclaimed communicator who has preached and taught in more than 75 nations across Africa, Asia, Europe, Latin America, the Middle East, and the USA. Key areas of emphasis include intimacy with God through the sanctifying power of the Holy Spirit, biblical leadership, discipleship, and missions.

Prior to establishing the International Leadership Institute, the Griffins served on the frontlines of Christian leadership development in the former Soviet Union. In the early 1990's, following the collapse of Soviet Communism, they served as missionaries in Estonia, establishing the Baltic Methodist Theological Seminary where Joy served on the faculty.

Joy is a graduate of the University of West Georgia and received the Master of Divinity degree from Asbury Theological Seminary. In 2004, Asbury Theological Seminary honored the Griffins as the first couple to receive the Distinguished Alumni Award. She also serves on the boards of Indian Springs Holiness Campmeeting, Francis Asbury Society, and Good News. Joy is joined in ministry by her husband, Wes, and their two children, Hannah and Caleb.

Joy's personal testimony is one of miraculous healing. After a devastating athletic injury, medical science deemed her condition impossible and incurable. But God . . . !!!

Thank you for taking the time to read *Jumping for Joy*!
I pray you were blessed and encouraged!

For more copies, or to contact me:
Facebook: Joy Smith Griffin
Email: Joy@iliteam.org

To invest in the ministry of Operation Beautiful Feet:
PO Box 1005
Carrollton, GA 30112

JAN DE CHAMBRIER

After a fulfilling career in music, God called Jan to full-time ministry in 2011 to express the love of Jesus to His children around the world through teaching, healing, and restoration. Serving as a Global Leader for International Leadership Institute, Jan has helped train indigenous Christian leaders in many different countries and wrote the *Healing and Restoration* curriculum for ILI's Leadership Beyond.

Jan serves as Director of International Healing Centers for Healing Tree International and has been designated a Global Leadership Ambassador through HTI. She is a recipient of the Golden Rule International Award from Ambassador Clyde Rivers. Together with her husband, Philippe, Jan founded the Christian Healing Prayer (CHP) ministry in 2013, establishing centers for healing prayer in hospital chapels in the greater Houston area. The de Chambriers also serve on the leadership team of Missional International Church Network (MICN) as Prayer Ambassadors. Joyfully married since 1988, they are the blessed parents of one son, Paul.

A frequent contributor to many publications, her articles appear in *Sharing* magazine as well as in online newsletters of MICN and the Holocaust Remembrance

Association. Jan's books include *Glimpses: Two Stories of Hope and Healing*, and *Greater Things than These: Practicing What Jesus Preached*. Having served on the faculty of the Shepherd School of Music at Rice University for 15 years prior to entering vocational ministry, Jan has produced two piano CDs, *In Perfect Peace* and *We are His People*.

For more information, please visit her website, www.glimpsesofhope.org.

Made in the USA
Columbia, SC
12 February 2021